THE LAWS AN ASS

A satirical look at the law, it's architects and practitioners

A memoir by

Doug Hemingway

Cover design by: Doug Hemingway

Disclaimer

All the opinions in this book are those of the writer alone. They do not necessarily reflect the views of the organisations to which he was affiliated. Nor does it reflect the opinions of the people with whom he worked.

None of the incidents referred to hereinafter have been taken from computer records. All of the stories come from the memory of the author. Although these stories are true to the best of his memory, names, places and times have been altered or simply not used. This is to protect the innocent and comply with the Data Protection Act.

All the different pieces of legislation were, to the best of the writer's knowledge, accurate at the time of writing. As legislation changes constantly to reflect changing attitudes, the writer cannot claim it will be accurate at the time of reading.

This body of work comes entirely from the writer's memory. The artwork comes from the author's own imagination. Any similarity to other images is purely co-incidental.

Table of Contents

Rules are for the obedience of fools and the guidance of wise men" – Harry Day

Introduction

<u>Health Warning</u>

What follows is a rant that includes opinions. Most are mine; some are other peoples'. There are also occasions where I would play devil's advocate to get a point across. If you are the type of person who believes that no one should hold opinions contrary to your own, then I would suggest that you stop reading this from here. Find a nice, uncontroversial romantic novel or a gentle autobiography. If on the other hand, you enjoy a debate, then do continue. There should be plenty here to grab hold of.

The law's an ass. What do we mean by this? Is it that the law is a beast of burden to be used by everyone in pursuance of whatever they happen to be pursuing? Is it simply a heteronym of that very beast and the part of the human anatomy normally kept covered in polite company? Yes, I am aware that it is a quote from the Dickensian character Mr Bumble. If memory serves, he was being told by a judge that the law supposed that he had dominion over his wife's actions and was therefore responsible for them. In reply he says, and I may be paraphrasing, that, "If the law supposes that, then the law is an ass...!" I do, however, believe that common usage rules. The meaning of quotes, idioms, proverbs, etc. are constantly changing to suit the modern world in which we live and the constantly changing language we use. Lawyers are always twisting the law around to suit their aims. To them, it would be like a beast of burden. Yet, to the public in general, the law must seem unbending. It could therefore be likened to the stubborn nature of an ass. Or we might believe that the law is idiotic and name it for what the Americans insist is called an 'ass'.

The following passage is about the strange ways in which laws are passed, interpreted and used by all practitioners. From the bobby on the beat to the crusty old appeal court Judge who is so far adrift from what is happening out in the big wide world, one wonders how he would be the appropriate person to make decisions in this field.

For anyone who has read my previous scratchings, there may be some examples in that volume that are similar to those I have used in this one. I'm just coming from a slightly different angle. I must also say that this is being written in the year 2020. A time of global upheaval with, thus far, an incurable viral pandemic raging around the globe. The pandemic has no bearing on what follows, but those conspiracy theories abound. The huge range of opinions being circulated has made it all too apparent that the public discourse is, ultimately that politicians, lawmakers and enforcers are getting it all wrong. I am therefore perhaps more conscious of the fact that should something I write become untrue or irrelevant, this is because laws change. Retrospective criticism is therefore pointless. That being said, I do love a good conspiracy theory if only for its comedic value.

I was a serving police officer for 30 years, the last 18 of which I was a detective investigating all manner of allegations. I spent the final eight years of my career investigating serious sexual assaults. I was at the coal face dealing with all aspects of the investigative process. From the initial report to the verdict at court, I made sure that, wherever possible, I was involved in all the decision-making processes for all the cases I investigated. I gained an in-depth knowledge of criminal legislation and the ways it is used and interpreted. It seems that the ones I got to know the best were the ones I think the legislators got wrong.

To understand where I am coming from in the pages that follow, we need to understand where our law comes from and who is responsible for making them. Is it the politicians, the majority of whom no one in their right minds would trust with anything at all much less the very bedrock of societal Britain? Or could it be the Civil Servants who appear to work entirely under the radar and who – at least as far as I can tell – are seldom particularly civil? Could it be the Police or even Johnny Public?

To put things into context, I will be using examples such as that of 'Johnny Public' mentioned above. As this could cross over into the realms of the dark and dingy world that is the Data Protection Act, I will not use real names, places, dates or times. The Data Protection Act is a much-maligned, misunderstood but essentially simple piece of legislation which tells us we can't bandy around the private details of other people held on computer. We can only have access to the information in limited circumstances. One of these circumstances is the prevention and detection of criminal offences – what I did. You don't want to breach the Data Protection Act. Judges can get really cross when that happens. Unless, of course, you are the CEO of Google (or any of the other tech groups who seem to take great pleasure in harvesting and selling our personal details). I only know this because I have noticed that if I take a look at a website selling beds, my computer gets filled inexplicably with ads for beds.

Civil servants, who have a high degree of legal training and experience, tend to be involved in the drafting of laws. Someone once told me that parliament is made up of failed lawyers and business people. Why go into a career that doesn't pay nearly as much as a lawyer can make unless you can't cut it in that environment. There are plenty of ex-politicians who do return to their previous lives. They are taken back because of the renewed personal profile enhancement that being a politician can bring, not to mention the contacts that they collect along the way. The theory appears to be borne out by the very nature of our laws. It would be very cynical of me to suggest that politicians draft laws that are deliberately porous, so that their mates, who are still working in the legal profession, can bamboozle ordinary people by their intellectual slights of hand, ably assisted by laws designed for that purpose. So I won't say that ... I will just leave it for other people to make their own minds up.

As far as Johnny Public and the police are concerned, this process is kept as far away from them as possible. The people used to make up laws all the time 1000s of years ago, right up until relatively recently. Common law is what everyday people and 'city elders' came up with to resolve disputes and create a society in which everyone could coexist happily (back when we didn't even have motors cars.) All of our legislation can be traced to common law except for the Road Traffic Act (RTA). We've only been driving cars for a hundred years or so. It didn't feature much in the conscience of King Arthur, Boudicca et al. Nothing was ever written down, nothing formalised. It was obvious things, like don't be a dick. Don't nick other people's gear, don't go around bashing people over the head with a big stick because you woke up on the wrong side of the bed. It was only when the law started being formalised that problems started happening. I know of only a few pieces of law that still use Common Law. Murder and Breach of the Peace are two of them. Both sit on opposite ends of the legal spectrum. They are both are shrouded in all sorts of codes of practice that are written down. There are also things like the power of entry to save life and limb. Most of these common-law things are augmented by enactments but are still in use to this day. Most of our laws are complied with, not out of blind obedience to the law, but due to most peoples' innate sense of right and wrong. Again, with the exception of the RTA. This is the most breached, ignored and reviled act of all. Because it isn't natural. There are few people on this planet who haven't breached an RTA rule.

Humans are pack animals in the same way as prides of lions, schools of dolphins and herds of antelope. We all have rules by which we are governed. If a member of the herd, school, pride or whatever you are a part of breaches those rules, the one doing the breaching is sanctioned (if caught – we know the first and last rule is 'don't get caught'). Now we know that if a lion breaks a rule, you won't have the lion elders all in a wood-panelled room, one with a silly long wig on, two with shorter silly wigs, a pasty-faced elder lion in his finest train-spotter accent explaining that, "Part A of Section 3, subsection 25b of the 'eating a carcass before daddy lion has had a go' act states, blah blah blah..." They have an innate knowledge of what they can and can't do. This is all taught to them by parents and other group members. They grow up knowing the rules.

It is no different with humans. We know not to steal, kill, hurt or damage from a very early age. The law tells us that anyone over the age of 10 is criminally responsible – with some caveats. We also know from a much earlier age where the line is drawn. The 'terrible twos' exist because we are starting to work out where the line is drawn and what the consequences of crossing that line are from that age. So we know the rules and what the consequences of breaking them are before we can even read.

We learn that one group of people who shouldn't have anything to do with the law has everything to do with it. We have learnt that those who it affects most, have little if anything to do with it and those who break the law know what they are doing most of the time. The bad news is that most people can do nothing about it. The good news is that it is such a mess that I have plenty to fill the pages hereinafter.

The Theft Act

Theft

Let us start with something nice and simple. The Theft Act describes theft as 'the dishonest appropriation of property belonging to another to permanently deprive the other of it.' Everyone knows what theft is. If you take some other bloke's stuff without his knowledge or permission and won't give it back, that is theft. Simple hey? Or is it? Seven sections in this one piece of legislation, six of which deal entirely with the meaning of each section of this pretty short sentence.

I will now introduce you to my first 'character' who will assist me in my explanations as clearly, and concisely as I can. Meet Johnny Joyrider – a misunderstood character at the best of times. He just likes to drive other people's cars and doesn't necessarily want to hang around to get their permission or go through all the hassle of getting insurance. It's far easier to hotwire the car, drive it around for a bit. Maybe get the Old Bill to chase him. Perhaps frighten the life out of a few little old ladies then dump and torch it on some open land.

So, Johnny Joyrider has nicked a car. Is this theft? 'Of course it is!' I hear you say. But is it? If Johnny doesn't get caught and then sells the car on, or destroys it, or at least tries to disguise its true identity, then yes, it is theft. If, however, he does get caught and says, "Sorry officer, I was only borrowing it, I was going to give it back honest, Guv." then can we prove that he intended to 'permanently deprive' the owner of it? If he hasn't changed the number plates and has made no effort to disguise the true origin of the car, then he can argue the point. It has been done plenty of times. Successfully.

So often, in fact, that they had to do something about the law. I don't think they felt they had to because people were wiggling out of theft charges. Lawyers and their political pals don't care about that. Getting people off, regardless of what their involvement may, or may not, have been is exactly what they do for a living. I think the problem was that it wouldn't even have been a fair fight. After all, some of those lawyers prosecute as well. So, Section 12 is created. This refers specifically to the taking of a motor vehicle or conveyance, it essentially removes the requirement to prove the 'permanent deprivation' element. It concentrates more on the sneakiness of the baddie. This is 'TWOCing' – or a TDA to the Met because the Met do everything differently – thus providing the police with an addition to their seemingly never-ending pool of acronyms and abbreviations.

It wasn't just car thieves. They also discovered that people were getting into taxis then running off without paying. Or eating meals in a restaurant then telling the waiter that they had no money to pay. This doesn't appear to be covered in The Theft Act as there is no property. It isn't as if the thief has taken the driver's or the restauranteur's money, it wasn't in their possession in the first place. Naturally, this merited an entirely new act. The Theft Act 1978. They still like the old one. It was, after all, only ten-years-old. It is porous and open to abuse, so they keep that in place and conveniently use the new as an 'add-on. This provides three new provisions, the first being a law of Making Off Without Payment – or in common parlance 'bilking' – then Evasion of Liability and finally Gaining Services by Deception.

The first and last are interesting. Making off without payment (Section 1) requires that the offender has used a legal service (Taxi ride or a meal in a restaurant for example) and has snuck off or ran away before the victim could take his cash. What the offender was getting had to be a legal service. A common phrase going around the shadier parts of London to do with ladies of the night falling victim of this little ruse was 'You can't bilk a bonk'. Because it was an illegal service, it couldn't come under Section 1. It is, however, a service. Whether or not it is legal, it is still a service, so you could prosecute under Section 3 - gaining services by deception. This one did not specify that requirement for the service to be legal. Of course, you'd still have to prove a deception, but I can't think of a single prosecution under this section of the act in terms of the services provided by ladies of the night. But hey, it's there. It would take a brave police officer to go with it.

Burglary

Let us try this one on for size. Surely no complications here Everyone knows what burglary is. Some bloke breaks your front window and has your telly away. A burglary, easy.

I will now introduce you to my second and third characters. Billy Burglar and Harry Housebreaker. I think it was their mother's fault that they kept getting caught. These are silly names to give people who want to go out stealing peoples' property for a living, who else are the police going to look for if you signpost their way to you like that. Perhaps it is nominative determinism, I don't know. At least we know that if they aren't illiterate, they are certainly alliterated.

There are two main parts to Burglary under Section 9 of the Theft Act 1968. Part A and part B. (they like simplicity sometimes)

The first is entering a premises as a trespasser intending to steal, seriously assault someone, damage property or rape someone. The second refers to where, having entered as a trespasser, one commits or attempts to commit theft or serious assault.

The more astute of you will have noticed a small anomaly here. In part b there is no mention of rape or damage. At the time of writing, a person convicted of theft could receive up to 7 years in prison. GBH would fetch ten years. Criminal damage could get you a life sentence, and so could Rape. The tariff for burglary itself was 14 years. It was therefore considered, that as Criminal damage and rape were more serious, it didn't need to be included, as the more serious offence would be charged. This all seems straight forward. But would I be writing it down if it was? Of course not!

Let's try to break it down. Criminal damage could mean anything from breaking a matchstick to burning down an entire row of houses without bothering to check if anyone is in there. I think we can all agree that someone who does the latter is going down for a long time. No one is going to give the former a second thought. GBH, on the other hand, requires two things that can be absent when it comes to criminal damage. Extreme violence, and the presence of the victim. Billy Burglar is a non-violent type. He just wants to nick your telly, flog it and get his next fix. He will want to make as much effort as he can to ensure he is not disturbed. He won't go in if he thinks that there is someone at home. He will plan an easy exit route in case there is. He probably won't even bother with deliberately causing damage. Not interested. He just wants to get in and out. Damage is only really caused when there are more than one of them, or they are in a derelict building where they're not expecting to be disturbed.

Most damage in these circumstances is minor. A bit of graffiti, and maybe the odd broken vase. All replaceable or repairable. GBH, on the other hand, requires someone else to be present. The violence can leave scars, physical or mental, that can't be erased. Especially if you take into consideration that the violence is in the victim's home, a place that they, hitherto, would have felt to be a safe place. There are also degrees of GBH. Anything from the cutting of all six layers of skin tissue to broken bones, concussions, life-endangering or life-changing injuries. Violence here is an essential ingredient.

Anyone who has been burgled will know of the anxiety that follows. Not feeling safe in your own home is a serious issue. If someone did break in and only caused a small amount of damage, he wouldn't be charged with burglary, but a low-level Criminal damage. But that feeling of insecurity will still be there, so why not treat the break-in on its merits?

Aggravated Burglary

I am led to this subject because I think the legislators got this entirely wrong. Aggravated burglary requires that, at the time of the offence, the burglar has in his possession, a 'weapon of offence.' It has nothing whatsoever to do with what happens during the burglary or even the intention of the burglar. Violence does not come into it as a factor, just the presence of a weapon. Here are some examples to demonstrate the ridiculous way in which this plays out in practice.

The first example will be demonstrated with the help of Billy Burglar. Billy breaks into a house by smashing a window to get in. He thinks that the place is empty and goes about his nefarious ways. As it happens, the occupier is at home. The occupant corners Billy burglar in the kitchen. Billy grabs a kitchen knife and stabs him, causing a serious injury. He makes good his escape with whatever property he can grab on the way out.

This is a straight-forward Burglary. He did not have the weapon at the time of the offence i.e. when the house was entered for the first time. He armed himself after he had initiated it.

The second example will be explained with the assistance of Harry Housebreaker. Harry is trying his hand at appropriating property from the house next door. He doesn't like confrontation. He just wants to get in and out as quickly as possible and flog whatever property he can, to get his next fix. To this end he decides a more silent approach to Billy is preferable, so he takes a flick knife with him to slip the sash window lock. He gains entry, nicks some jewellery and scarpers, unseen.

This is aggravated burglary. The law states that a flick knife has only one use – that of a weapon. Never mind the electrician working on an overhead power line who needs to easily open and close the knife that he uses in his work and will often have only one free hand. Or the intention of the burglar in this instance. But the law is the law. Harry has, in his possession, at the time of committing burglary, a weapon. His offence is therefore deemed more serious than Billy's in terms of the break-in.

I know that judges have discretion. They can take many factors into account when passing down sentences, but you see what my issues are.

Let's take Billy's indiscretion and see how we can develop it. We will change the circumstances a little. Everything is the same until he is confronted in the kitchen. Only this time, our occupant is a little lighter on his feet, and he avoids the knife by retreating out of the kitchen into the lounge. This is Billy's escape route, so he has no option but to follow him into the lounge. He still has the knife on him and threatens the occupant to progress to his escape route. The occupant complies. Billy grabs a mobile phone from the coffee table on his way out and makes good his escape. No injuries are sustained by any party apart from the bruising to the occupant's pride.

This is aggravated burglary. When billy moves into the lounge, this is a separate part of the house and a 'new' trespass. So, he has his weapon as he enters this part of the house as a trespasser. He is using it to threaten the occupant, so it is an 'offensive weapon' that he has on him at the time of the offence. He is also in there to steal, not to injure. Yet this is still, somehow, more serious than the first example I gave?

Surely one's intentions should be at the forefront of aggravating factors. I think this is non-sensical.

Let us try a slightly different scenario. One that happens from time to time. The local tramp decides that he needs to get out of the rain to get his head down after a busy day of begging. He finds a derelict building and decides that this is his palace for the night. There are our two burglar brothers to consider. They are in the habit of roughing him up every now and then for a bit of sport, so our itinerant friend picks up a scaffolding pole on his way in. He intends to protect himself against attack as he tries to get a little shut-eye.

As it happens Billy and Harry have seen him go in. They make plans to go in there a little later and give him a good old shoeing. Break a few bones. See how loudly he squeals, maybe nick today's takings – just a bit of fun. So later on, they go into the building to look for him. Our itinerant friend hears them come in and slips into another room in the hope that they will go away. They don't. They enter the room in which our tramp is concealed to do as they planned. As they enter, the tramp takes a swing at one of them breaking a bone in Billy's hand. He then does a runner in the ensuing confusion.

In conclusion, it seems that Billy and Harry, should they have legitimate access to the building, have committed no offence. Barring a potential conspiracy to cause grievous bodily harm (although, good luck with that.) They are not trespassers. This means they are not burglars in this instance. But, if they can be shown as trespassers, this would be straight burglary if you can prove the intention to gbh or thieve.

Our itinerant friend may be in for a few more problems. His intension when first entering the building was not to steal, or anything of the like, so he is, at this point guilty only of civil trespass. Not covered in criminal legislation. Even when he takes the weapon, if his intension was to threaten, there is no burglary. The legislation does not mention threats. Indeed there are no offences at all because although the pole is a weapon for his purposes, the building is not a public place and the act that deals with offensive weapons, requires it to take place in a public space. He is, however, a trespasser. So when he does seriously injure Billy, (broken bone) while having a weapon on him, it is aggravated burglary.

I will now show an example from my own experience to put these examples into 'real-life context'

I was dealing with an incident where someone was arrested for aggravated burglary during the night. I came to work in the morning to be presented with the allegation and was tasked to deal with the incident and the person who was in custody. I later realised that I had dealt with the detainee about a year earlier. That was a simple enquiry and nothing to do with what happened the night before. I found her to be a perfectly decent, well-adjusted individual at that time, so I found it odd that this would have happened. I went to the scene with a colleague to investigate and this is what I found:

Since I had last seen the person, a new family had moved into the flat immediately above her. The entrances to both flats were on the ground floor. Both front doors led out onto a small, shared entrance passage. It was no more than a metre or so square and opened out onto the pavement. The doors were next to each other. Her door led straight into her flat. The other opened onto a flight of stairs to the flat above. This new family were a well-known family of thugs who were a blight on any neighbourhood they went into. They had obviously played their music at full volume until 4am every morning and didn't care that no one was getting any sleep. It got to the point where the woman on the ground floor started suffering mentally. She couldn't get any sleep; she couldn't concentrate at work. Her life and mental health were being adversely affected. On this evening she'd had enough. She grabbed a heavy axe handle or some such weapon that she had behind her front door. She went out of her door and, seeing that the neighbour's door was insecure from the numerous times that the police had been a little overzealous in their knocking at the door, she simply pushed the door open and went up the stairs wielding the weapon, and entered the room. In fairly forthright terms, she explained to them within which orifices the weapon would end up should they continue making her life hell. She may even have used the odd expletive and may have even raised her voice! She then turned and went back to bed, leaving the weapon behind her door where she had always kept it. Police were called and she was arrested for aggravated burglary. After a little more investigation, we returned to the station and released the detainee.

No burglary – aggravated or otherwise – was committed. She was not an invited guest, so she was certainly a trespasser. Her intention on entry was to shout at them. She made threats, but the act does not cover threats, only intention. There is an offence of making threats to assault, but this has to be an immediate threat without conditions. The theory being, if you don't want to be assaulted, then perhaps don't do what you are doing. So, all you are left with is the possession of an offensive weapon, but that can only happen in a public place, of which the flat is not. Even the threatening behaviour, which would be covered by the public order Act has to be committed when at least one of the parties is in a public place. So she walked out of the police station, reputation intact, a little frazzled but at least a little more rested. We like to think we provided a service.

I really felt for this woman. It must have taken a lot for a perfectly reasonable, level-headed person to go to the lengths that she did.

Fraud

We now turn to fraud, or deception, or artifice. Conmen, grifters, swindlers, fraudsters. It doesn't matter what you call it or them. It is just nicking stuff using a different method. That's why it comes under The Theft Act. The act drones on about all sorts of things, but when it comes down to it, if someone makes you believe one thing when it isn't true, and as a result, the person manages to relieve you of property or cash, that is deception. We all know how to deceive; we have all been doing it from the moment we could talk. It's just that most of us either choose not to because we have grown out of it and we don't need to con mummy into believing that we need an ice cream anymore. Or we do not have the wherewithal to bamboozle (the latter would describe me perfectly).

Most con artists will want you to believe that they only deceive dishonest people. This is rather simplistic and not always the case. Yes, there are many scams out there that convince you that you are getting something for nothing, or at least very little. The person is preying on greed to get what they want. So it does happen, but I have dealt with plenty of people who just wanted to put their savings or their personal property somewhere safe for the benefit of their family. When these people get conned, it is sad. The proliferation of internet scams has shattered this romantic view of conmen. It started out as someone suggesting that if you were to accept a load of cash into your account for them to slip it past HMRC, then they will leave a little gift when they withdraw it. Now they don't even bother, they just nick your online details by persuading you that they are some sort of official, then clean you out. They don't care if you are poor or rich, nor good or bad, they are faceless people who don't want to work for a living.

The Brighton Knockers are probably the most infamous group of con artists. They all came from the Hove area (right next to Brighton, hence the name) and operated the Greater London and Home Counties area. What they did was to go to well-to-do houses, preferably owned by little old ladies and offer to buy their furniture. They would go into the house and spot something that was going to be a big money-spinner. They would then direct their attention away from the item and concentrate on some tat that wasn't that expensive. They would offer a price that was well in excess of what it was worth and then say. "I'll do you a favour," And while turning to what they actually want very badly continue, "I'll take this old bit of rubbish off your hands as well. Looks like its only cluttering up your hallway. I'll tell you what, I won't even charge for the removal" They then get a £100 piece of furniture that they paid £500 for and a £5000 piece of furniture that they paid nothing for. Of course, if they didn't get their way, they would just send someone back when the house was unoccupied and nick it anyway. Now, while they justified themselves by telling the world that the victims were wealthy and could afford it, sometimes it wasn't about the money. Sentimental value is not replaceable. Being conned like this often leaves a mental scar and an inability to trust people. It also does affect the 'man on the Clapham omnibus' – that mythical person that law-makers like to refer to in order to describe the ordinary man in the street – because insurance companies charge their rates to offset losses such as these. So your insurance premiums and mine are influenced by big payouts. And big payouts go to people who are wealthy enough to have expensive tat that insurance companies have to fork out for. So don't believe these self-serving little ne'er-do-wells, they are conning you... again.

For the old fashioned grifter, it was all about smoke and mirrors. Leaving trails that lead up blind allies. Getting people to look at this hand while that one did the dirty. I investigated what was probably the first case that came out on the back of the 2012 Olympics. The man just couldn't help himself. I worked out that he must have been planning it all while he was serving time for another fraud. He came out of prison and within a week, he had obtained a credit card in a false name (he had so many different identities that he'd probably forgotten his own name). Within the month, he had hired office space and fully furnished without parting with a bean. By the end of the second month, he had taken on staff, whom he never paid. He then set up a website, persuaded several very high profile athletes to endorse his scam, and then started preying on the parents of up-and-coming athletes, who would never quite make the grade, with promises of advertising contracts and endorsements as well as a place in the London 2012 Olympics. I believe he ended up having to part with about £2000 when the scam started to come apart. But this guy managed to con businessmen, high profile athletes with coaches and lawyers without parting with anything at all. All to relieve hard stretched proud parents of their hard-earned for his own greed. Just getting my head around the sheer size of the scam was hard enough. The paperwork was vast. Everything led to fresh air. This wasn't about preying on the greed of the victims, this was about preying on the hopes and wishes of proud parents who were giving up everything for the benefit of their offspring. He shattered many dreams. I have no doubt that he is once again preparing his next scam while serving out his sentence for that one.

The lesson this individual in particular needed to learn – other than don't con people – was that if you're going to hire staff, pay them. Loyalty is in short supply when you don't pay. Especially when you have never known them before.

But why is fraud quite so rife? The reason is that it isn't sexy enough for politicians to get hot under the collar about it. Politicians see it as a victimless crime as the banks just payback losses (most of the time). I used to investigate this sort of stuff. When it involves credit card fraud, the banks have to provide bank details. The banks don't like giving up clients details even when there is clear evidence that a crime has been committed. So the investigation was always difficult. Banks made information hard to come by. Eventually, it was decided that we would tell the bank that a fraud was committed and get them to put the evidence together, send us the results of their sleuthing so that we could complete our side of the investigation and hopefully prosecute offenders.

Now, the Home office has put all credit card investigations into the banks' hands. If you go to the police station to report a credit card fraud, they will just refer you to your bank. This is not the police being lazy, it is official policy. This suits the politicians as the crime isn't recorded unless there is sufficient evidence to charge someone. So fewer recorded crimes and higher 'clear-up' rates. It also suited the banks because all they had to do, was maintain high bank charges to offset their losses, then just not bother to investigate anything other than the most serious occurrences – or anything where the bank could not cover their losses in bank charges. So we know that there is a lot of fraud out there. But ask a politician and he will tell you that it is much better than it was. It isn't. It's worse. It just isn't going through the system like it used to.

Of course, the internet is always going to be the fraudster's best friend. They used to have to get in peoples' faces to get them to part with their goods. Now, because we have all given up our privacy for the convenience of the internet, they can be faceless, nameless and come from anywhere in the world all from their bedroom. They don't prey on greedy people any more. They don't assess whether or not the victim can afford to lose a few bob. They just want your money and if that means they are rich and you are destitute, so what!

How many of us have had a text message saying something to the effect of, "This is HMRC. You are being investigated for tax evasion. Press 1 to make contact with us. If you don't, a warrant will be issued, and you will be arrested." I have, several times. My advice is, bin it! Do not open it, do not telephone the number, do not think about it, just bin it. If the HMRC were investigating you, for a start you will probably be aware that you are doing something dodgy and if you aren't, then why bother? Secondly, they would never tell you about it until they are knocking at your door. They certainly wouldn't send you a text. This one is definitely not preying on your greed, just your fear of the authorities. The authorities aren't something to fear, they just want what they believe you owe. If they can get the money without resorting to the hassle of court appearances and warrants and all that boring stuff, they are happy, it means they don't have to investigate it anymore. That being said, they will go for the easier target. Big corporations will just put everything through their solicitors who will fight tooth and nail for every penny. The little one-man-band who runs a small High Street outlet, won't have that facility and will normally do as they are told. So, unfortunately, they will be targeted.

Robbery

I will deal with this subject later on under a different heading as different aspects of the way we deal with things arise in this subject. My fourth and final Character, Rodney Robber will rear his ugly head then. This is a cocky little ne'er-do-well, who bravely picks on people younger and smaller than himself only when he's backed up by his little posse of thugs.

I did hear of one occasion when a young man of this ilk went into a pub. He was known by the locals to live and operate. He went into the toilet to recycle his beer intake and was followed in by another unidentified man. This second man said to Rodney Robber, "Are you the boy who is going around robbing little old ladies?" (he may have used slightly different language incorporating a few choice Anglo-Saxon phrases). Rodney said, (again using slightly less-than-polite language) "What's it to you...?" He wasn't able to finish his sentence. He woke up three days later in hospital resolutely not wanting to talk to police or press charges.

I shouldn't advocate summary justice, but sometimes...

Marché Oeuvre

This is a concept that is no longer valid, but I have had someone use it as a defence many years ago. The concept is that proprietary rights to stolen property cannot be transferred purely by buying the item. If police stopped a man riding a £2000 bicycle and the rider states that he bought it for £50 off his mate, suspicions would rightly be aroused. If the victim of the theft could be found, he would get his bike back – eventually. But it used to be, in days of yore, that in certain open-air markets, between the hours of sunrise and sunset, items could legitimately be bought and sold with impunity. This all happened hundreds of years ago when people tended to stay in the area in which they lived – airports in Henry VIII's time were relatively ill-equipped. People didn't tend to travel quite so much. It was therefore felt that if property was stolen, it would almost certainly be sold in a local market as that was the only place that would get rid of things that thieves wanted to be rid of. If the victim of theft did not go to their local market to try to find their property, they were not showing sufficient diligence. Stolen items could therefore be exchanged, and it was considered that proprietary rights would then be properly transferred. So, when I approached a well-known local thief, circa 1990, wearing a very expensive leather jacket that he had just stolen from an exclusive Kings Road shop in Chelsea, he said, "I bought in an open-air market during daylight hours." Although this happened 30 years ago, I am fairly confident that this statement is verbatim, it was a set script that these sorts of people used. He didn't get away with it.

Sexual Offences

This is a field within which I worked for around eight years. I have, therefore, unsurprisingly, developed strong opinions towards what the law surrounding it encompasses. The following chapter touches upon some manifestly sensitive and bleak issues. In this spirit, I want to reiterate the tone in which this monologue has been written. I want to shine a light on the legislation, the way it is dealt with by various legal agencies, and in turn, provide objective criticism of how this can reflect incorrectly upon the offence and those it affects.

There is a lot of rubbish spoken about this subject. These views are often based on ignorance or personal and cultural beliefs. Many of which are not only contrary to the laws of this land, but also to my personal, moral compass. In the world of police investigations, major crimes like murder and organised crime are dealt with by teams of officers. Each incident has a whole team to deal with particularities, with a Detective Inspector (DI) heading it up. In the criminal sphere of rape and serious sexual offences, where the only crime officially considered more serious is murder, you get one detective; one constable; and the rest is supervised by other ranks. For completeness, the constable is the first point of contact and is a highly skilled position – make no mistake. So when I investigated one of these crimes, it was me and the victim liaison only. Not some other senior ranking officer.

There is, unfortunately, still a stigma attached to the subject of sexual offences. The law was changed in 2003 from a load of bits and pieces of law, some of which were ludicrously outdated. Some were simply intellectually misinformed. For example, it was written into law that a 12-year-old boy could not attain an erection, and therefore, it was impossible for him to commit rape. How stupid is that? What it means is that you could have been a witness to a vicious rape by a boy of 11 years and 11 months old and you would be able to do virtually nothing about it, bar informing the social services. So, because it was written into legislation, it was so. No sane person believes that sexual maturity can only be attained after 12, surely. Yet there it is, codified and clear as day. Let's not even consider those members of our varied community who have no birth certificates or any formal proof they exist. All they would have to say is that they are under 12. What could the police do about that? Some do reach sexual maturity early, so how can a law override reality? Thus, one can begin to understand the decision to overhaul the legislation in 2003, aiding consistency and dragging us, kicking and screaming into the 21st century.

It wasn't just the law that was overhauled. In an ideal world, all victims of domestic violence would leave their partners, and all aggressors would be prosecuted. However, despite consensus within the system, we do not live in an ideal world. The new system, therefore, attempted to deal with these issues. In many ways they succeeded but, as in all things, it was never going to be perfect. The way police investigated rape went through a huge sea-change. Even in my earlier times in the service, it wasn't unusual to hear police officers telling the victim of an extremely violent husband that it wasn't a matter for the police. It was her word against his. She should either leave the man, or 'put up and shut up.' It was determined that this should never happen again.

Paedophilia. I need not elaborate. Children used to be told that they were imagining things when they alleged sexual assaults. It wasn't just the police either. It was parents, teachers, social services, the entire adult population let our kids down. Who could kids go to if their Mother told them not to make up stories, or their teachers just dismissed them? The same goes for mentally ill people. They were simply ignored. Our handling of cases where women were attacked after spending the evening in a pub was less than satisfactory. These people were told to simply take more care of themselves. All this just meant that men – and it was men for the most part – were able to do what they wanted and get away with it.

Fortunately, that all changed. We set up units that specialised in dealing with these allegations. We worked out how to compile evidence from kids and mentally ill people that could withstand the rigours of being tested in court. Methods that included obtaining statements without leading the victim in any way so that we could show the court that the information was from the victim alone and not augmented by incomplete investigations.

Suspension of Belief

As in most things, they didn't get it all right. Because it was believed that we, the police, were disbelieving our victims, they set about changing the attitudes. It wasn't entirely true that we didn't believe them. I think it was just a case of not believing that they could prove an offence where you only have one person's word against another.

It is true that a court case probably wouldn't get past the first hurdle if all you had was one word against another. The trick was to carry on digging. One would often hear detectives expressing disbelief in the victim's account, but I think this was a defence mechanism. Rightly or wrongly, this was probably because they felt powerless in lacking the authority they were granted to change the fact that the victim, by law, was not protected.

What actually happened was that the senior officers decided that police would believe all victims. At first glance, this appears ok. But it isn't. People can lie. Whether we want to hear this or not, they do. Sometimes, people can merely remember incorrectly. Though rare, we mustn't turn a blind eye to even the smallest number of cases in which injustice can occur in such a way. Often it is a case of interweaving the truth with lies. What the hierarchy did was to tell us to believe everyone, regardless of how factually accurate they were being. No one can instruct me to believe a lie. Nor can anyone instruct me to ignore what evidence had told me was true. So what do we do about it? Ignore senior officers and politicians? Probably not a good idea. Detectives have a mantra they always used: 'believe no one, question everything.' It may sound quite stark, but if you stuck to that, then you could never be accused of being biased, and you would only ever believe something if evidence allowed. Obviously, you don't say that out loud or even give that impression. Everyone wants to be believed, even liars – especially liars – so it comes as a shock when your information isn't swallowed unquestioningly. We just need to understand that it is for a good reason.

The answer was fairly easy. I took the view that I would collect information from as many sources that I could. I would not challenge that information initially, I would simply gather it. I could then compare accounts. I could use irrefutable evidence such as DNA records, CCTV, physical injuries and such like. I would then be able to build a picture and believe whatever the facts told me to believe. I then couldn't be accused of being biased towards one party or the other. If the facts suggested that someone wasn't entirely honest – be they victims, witnesses or suspects – we would be duty-bound to 'clarify' the information. It wasn't unusual for me to conduct more than one interview of a suspect or witness. The second was usually challenging the person's initial account. This would've been because I had discovered a lie. The most interviews I have conducted with one person in a single case was five. This got quite complicated as there were five suspects initially, and most were interviewed at least twice. Three were eventually charged and two convicted.

There was a recent case where a man accused prominent politicians of being involved in paedophile rings. The allegations were ultimately discredited, and the media were all over it like a cheap suit. Politicians were apparently horrified and protesting innocence loudly ... and regularly. They would have shouted it from the rooftops if they thought it would help. When senior police officers were asked about the case by the media, they simply told the press that police 'always believe the victim.' Well, needless to say, this went down like a lead balloon. How can the police do that, they are meant to be 'impartial'. They were dragging the good name of public servants through the mud because they believed an uncorroborated account from an untested witness over an upstanding public servant. It was a mess. The man making the allegations was eventually investigated and found to be guilty of lying to the police.

I don't know the truth of the matter. Some may say that the political machine went into the overdrive and evidence was 'found' to discredit the man. I don't know. It wouldn't be the first time, but, as it stands, the man was discredited. What do we think the police did about this policy of 'always believing the victim'? Nothing. Despite being ridiculed, the senior officers continued with the same line, and to my knowledge still do to this day. That is not to say the people doing the actual investigations held the same view. Most did what I did and followed the evidence. When a boss wanted to stick their oar in, we would just tug our forelock, say, "yessir, of course, sir, whatever you wish sir." Then go off and effectively ignore what was said and investigate the allegation properly.

Lies, Damned Lies and Statistics

They say that about 3% of rape allegations are ever convicted at court. I am pleased to say that my success rate was well above that, but that number taken in isolation means very little. We have to consider the other 97%. How many were investigated to find that no offences have been committed in law? There are many reasons for this, ranging from the victim lying, (either partially or wholly), to the victim simply misunderstanding what rape actually is. It might sound strange, but it does happen. Often the victim decides that they don't want to go ahead with the allegation. If we have no victim – and there are rarely witnesses – then we have no case. We then need to look at whether there was ever any chance of finding the culprit. Perhaps it was a historical allegation and the suspect was dead or unidentifiable. There are some cases that the Crown Prosecution Service (CPS) refuses to charge. Again, there are different reasons for this that I will go into later. What I will say, is that if I've investigated an incident and can give you chapter and verse about what happened, when it happened and how it happened, yet it doesn't go to court for purely political reasons, one can hardly blame the investigation. Add to that the fickle nature of juries in these cases and the fact that some people are acquitted because the jury will have been prevented from hearing all the evidence. Some jurors also won't convict due to, for example, cultural considerations. It happens far too often. Yes, and there are investigations that police just simply do a bad job of. That happens as well.

So throwing around random figures doesn't really help. It is much more complicated than that, and so much more complicated than what the media would have you believe.

Domestic Rape

Let us deal with domestic rape. It is an indisputable fact that abusive relationships include sex as part of the stick the abuser uses to 'beat' the victim. In the majority of cases, it is the man in the relationship that is the abuser, and he will use rape as one of the tools in his armour to subjugate his victim. We should remind ourselves that rape is not about sex, it is about power, the removal of choice and control. So it stands to reason that in a violent relationship – which is always about power, the removal of choice and control – the abuser is always going to resort to this. The problem is finding out when it is happening. The victims are more often than not made to believe that no one will listen to them, and even if they did, no one else would want them afterwards. They are often isolated from all friends and family, so there is no one to advise them otherwise. They are trapped.

When they do eventually come forward, it can often be relatively straight forward, if a little labour intensive, to prove historical abuse (old injuries, medical records genital wounds, the abuser's propensity towards violence etc.) We will build a picture that will lead us toward certain conclusions. But we have to be realistic. We can't use DNA if they are living together and there are never witnesses. We also have other issues that we have to get around. The lucky ones may be able to speak to a friend who convinces them to make the allegation. But this can generate its own problems. The victim will tell the friend that her partner wanted sex, so she agreed to avoid a violent incident. When we dig deeper, we sometimes find that at the time, the man was being perfectly level headed. The problem was that she knew that if she said no, he would have flown into one, so she just agreed. What is tragic is that we cannot prove rape. We know that the man knows he is violent. He knows that she is only agreeing to his demands because that she just wants a quiet life. But we have to operate on facts, and we can't tell a jury that the man could read the woman's mind. When all is said and done, she has to say no, or at least give clear, unambiguous signals that she is not up for it. If she even meekly agrees, it is not rape. It will always be recorded as rape in the system and the investigation will be shown as a failure. We cannot, however, twist the law to suit us. That is for lawyers and politicians to do. That is their job.

I have examples of successes and failures, but they don't really add to the conversation. I did have one where the attacker had to physically drag her trousers down while she fought to keep them on. We could prove forensically that her account was probably accurate. This, in itself, would not help much. What did help, was that the same forensic exam could prove beyond doubt that the attacker's account was not truthful. One-nil to police. I think that case succeeded because the jury, despite vociferous arguments from the defence team, was allowed to hear the 999 recording and that just broke everyone's hearts. No one could fake that.

There are several other issues with this subject. There are many people out there – including some women – who just don't believe that domestic rape is a 'thing'. And there is usually no persuading them otherwise. We also have to be aware that some victims will lie. I have known cases where an allegation was made against a husband only to find that after an extensive investigation, it was the wife who was the abuser, and the husband was unwilling or unable to admit this fact. It is rare, but it happens. We also have to consider those who leave bits of information out in the hope that we won't find out. Maybe another man was on the scene or involvement with illicit drugs. It is all very well, and it may not have anything to do with the allegation. But try to tell the defence that. So, any information that is found has to be disclosed. If it has been withheld by the victim, the defence would go into overdrive and trash everything because, "if she lied about this, what else is she lying about? We have to assume that she has never told the truth from that start!" The case then gets dumped by the CPS, and the police get blamed for failing in their investigation. The same does not go for the defendant. He can lie through his back teeth, change his mind, do whatever he wants. The legal system will not sanction him. His evidence may be seen less sympathetically by the jury, but sometimes it may not.

I say all this, not to give the impression that I don't believe a word anyone says, nor do I wish to give the impression that I hear an allegation and hold no views on it whatsoever. We are human, after all. We have our own minds and a natural inclination to form an opinion when hearing a story. The trick is to override opinion, follow protocol, do the investigation, and only believe what the facts direct you so to do. There are several occasions where a full investigation has proved my initial assessment wrong. And this goes in both directions – believing the victim to find out it was all a tissue of lies, and other times not believing the victim to find that their account was, in fact truthful. This can only happen if the investigator follows protocol, suspends belief and follows the evidence. In subjects such as these, there is so much in the way of judgemental attitudes, that victims shy away from the whole truth. I had a case where a woman was abused by a very violent ex-husband who walked around in a bulletproof vest due to the company he kept. I absolutely believed everything she had told me. Unfortunately, she forgot to tell me that she had called her grown-up sons at the time of the incident and they had come and chased him away, armed to the teeth with I-dread-to-think-what. The problem was that I had to disclose the findings. If I had found the information, the defence could do the same. I would then be accused of being dishonest in my investigation. When I did, the CPS dropped the case like a hot potato. A very violent thug still walks the street as a result.

Mental Health Issues

And what of mental illness? These are people who are targeted by abusers. The abusers believe that everyone will believe them over the 'nutter', and they invest a lot of time and effort convincing the victims that this will happen. I'm not saying that just because someone has a mental difficulty, we should believe everything they say. We just have to be very careful about how we gather evidence. We shouldn't dismiss them out of hand. However, we have to be aware that they are vulnerable and are, therefore, targets for horrible people to take advantage of. When a woman once made an allegation that the occupant of the flat one floor below her had raped her daily over a long period of time, we took notice. When the entire story came out, it was discovered that he had never actually entered her flat nor she, his. It was all done telepathically through the floorboards. Sad but true. We can obviously do nothing with that sort of allegation. Of course, it will remain on the system as a failed investigation, but no one is going to have their good name besmirched.

What we have to do with many people with mental difficulties is to have 'psych assessments.' We need to find out what the mental age is. This is not an exact science, but we know when we are speaking to someone who has no idea what sex is all about, nor what the consequences of the sexual act can be. If we can prove that the person has a mental age of below 12, especially when they are in their twenties and above, then we should treat them as if they were under that age, with all that entails within the law. For all the posturing of the abusers trying to convince us that the accuser is not of sound mind, if we can prove sexual contact, the abusers have to show that they believed the person to be of sound mind. It is incumbent upon the person of sound mind to be the adult in all respects. This obviously causes them a problem – he can shout from the rooftops that the person making the allegation is completely insane, but he would then have to explain why he took advantage. They might even try to convince us that the person is sane and then try to deal with the allegation at hand. Tough one, but the easiest way to do it, is leave well alone. Of course, if the mental age is above 12, we have to deal with it so much more carefully. They are no more or less vulnerable to abusers, but if they are shown to have the mental capacity to make these decisions, then we have no choice but to deal with them as adults. The mental issues would then be dealt with as appropriate.

There are so many factors to take into account when dealing with this subject. What it all comes down to is:

Can we show consent was either never given or withdrawn at any point?

How was that lack of consent conveyed to the attacker?

Did the attacker know what was or wasn't being consented to?

What did the attacker do that contravened the wishes of the victim?

Once these questions have been satisfactorily answered, everything else is just padding.

Public Order

By and large, the politicians don't really want to touch this. The legislation, when it comes down to it, essentially says be reasonable and 'don't be a dick'. It can, however, get very political when it comes to racial and cultural concerns. Let's face it, it has to make a person worse if he is a racist dick.

There is a book that came out at the turn of the millennium, that is a pictorial chronicle of the second millennium. My ugly mug can be found in this rather weighty tome, pictured during the poll tax disturbances in London. This was the first time that I came up against the political machine at it's finest.

I'll be long-winded about this. I have to fill these pages with something after all. The Public Order Act was enacted a year before I joined the police. It has therefore been in the system for the entire length of my service. All the legal boffins put their heads together, to come up with something that made it illegal to be a dick in public. The phrase that they liked was 'harassment, alarm and distress'. This phrase is peppered throughout the piece of legislation.

What they also did was decide at what level something took a step up from being an idiot in public to being a threatening idiot in public, to a bunch of people being threatening idiots in public ... and so on. What they came up with, using all the scientific brainpower at their disposal, was that it took at least 12 people to cause a riot. This didn't even come from them. Their predecessors in the 18th century decided this when penning The Riot Act. They just followed suit. They believed that regardless of the size of the crowd, it is 12 people or more who could cause pandemonium. Any less, then it is 'violent disorder'. Now I am sure if we look at studies around herd mentality, 'ripple effects' and the like there is probably something in it but surely, it can't be quite so black and white.

Riot

To have a riot, you have to have '12 or more persons who are present together using or threatening unlawful violence for a common purpose and the conduct of them (taken together) is such as would cause a person of reasonable firmness present at the scene to fear for his personal safety, each of the persons using unlawful violence for the common purpose is guilty of riot.'

This is alphabet soup! Let me put this in a way we can all understand. A group of thugs decide they want to disrupt a peaceful demo. They are just about to go out when they realise that there are 12 of them. They all stop in their tracks and decide who is going to have to drop out. Heaven forbid they are all captured! That would be accused of causing a riot! We can't have that! One of them then pipes up and says, "I'll tell you what, you 11 go out and cause problems. I come with you, but I will be causing problems for an entirely different reason. I will present together with you, but I will not be acting for a common purpose." Everyone breathes a sigh of relief and go out happy in the knowledge that they aren't rioting. Sensible hey?

But it gets worse. The precursor to the Public Order Act was a bunch of bits of legislation and common law. Most have heard the phrase 'reading the Riot Act.' The Riot Act of 1714 provided the power to local authorities to disperse crowds of 12 or more who were causing problems. They would be required to read a script telling everyone to sod off or get nicked. They would then post it around the place and, like a game of hide-and-seek, count down, then shout 'coming! ready or not!' then arrest everyone who hadn't taken the hint. The system worked well.

In our modern, shiny world, it has to be 'declared' a riot by the Home Secretary. So never mind all the words and bumph that accompany the legislation. No one really needs to know it at all. Apart from the Home Secretary. Now all you have to do is get a politician to make a decision. Don't hold your breath.

Let's return to my moment in the spotlight in this chronicle. I was a young, uniformed officer assigned, along with half the Met, to police the demonstration of people shouting about the newly enforced Poll Tax. We were all briefed and told that it would be a nice gentle family day out. Grannies and Grandpas would be out and about with their little grandchildren and puppy dogs. Butterflies would be fluttering in the flowers and little lambs would be gambolling in the park. An idyllic family day out. Everyone was going to have fun, fun, fun. Oh, and there may be some small scuffles caused by a tiny minority of three thousand people! Three thousand thugs who want to disrupt this march! Not 12 – because that is all you'd need to disrupt a demo – no, three THOUSAND! So, we were all sent out like lambs to the slaughter. We were unarmed and unprotected – no ballistic or stab-proof vests in those days. The unit that was set up to deal with mass disturbances was on duty but were actually told not to deploy when the brown stuff started to hit the fan. The senior officers wanted the public to see that the police were not the aggressors, so they sat and watched as we got our behinds delivered to us on a plate. Missiles were thrown, cars torched and buildings looted. Utter mayhem. It was in those circumstances, lined up with a load of other officers, that I was snapped by some sort of photographer. The picture then found it's way into the *Chronicle of Britain and Ireland*.

On the positive side, we were able to test out these brand new high visibility vests. Police had never used them before. Not many were using them on the day. The guys in my unit were. They worked well, the 'rioters' could spot us from a mile off. They could aim all manner of missiles at us.

To top it all, I went to public order training about a month later and was told that senior police and politicians believed that the operation was a success! (They missed out 'but the patient died' part of the phrase.) The politician in charge never declared it a riot. This was because he couldn't prove that more than 12 people were present together. Blah, blah, blah. I don't care what he or anyone else thought, that was the dictionary definition of a riot. It was also the dictionary definition of an abject failure in terms of the operation. They failed us, they failed the peaceful demonstrators, they failed everyone. But hey, their offices were air-conditioned and comfortable – so, all good.

Of course, in our brave new world, we have now found out why these events aren't classified as riot. If they were, then the government would be liable for damage reparations. How much easier is it to say, "Nah, not a riot mate. Just a disturbance. Don't call us, we'll call you."

Breach of the peace

I was involved in an interesting use of a 'breach of the peace' once. An unfortunate man had been taken to the police station due to his highly erratic and threatening behaviour. The police station in these circumstances is viewed as a place of safety. The police station in these circumstances is viewed as a place of safety, and the police have the power to remove anyone who is deemed to be vulnerable to such a place. A hospital would, in these circumstances be better as a place of safety. However, for reasons no one really got to the bottom of, the officers dealing with him felt that the police station was the best place to take him. It was determined by the custody staff that he was not in his right mind. He did not know whether he was coming or going. Legislation affords us the opportunity to detain people under the Mental Health Act for 72 hours in order to get a proper mental health assessment, for the person to be dealt with appropriately. This has to be done by two independent mental health doctors separately. The first one came along, did his assessment and declared him as mad as a march hare. The second one showed up a few hours later and said that he was perfectly fine. He tossed him a tenner so he could get back to his hometown in Brighton, so off he toddled. Two hours later, I came across him about 500 yards from the police station from which he had been released. He was raging and threatening and scaring the life out of the well-to-do residents of the area in which I worked. He was clearly in a state of mental break-down, and it was decided that he should be taken straight to a hospital this time to be properly assessed. The theory here is that doctors at a police station would just think that the person they are there to assess, isn't in a hospital, so it isn't their problem. Take him to a hospital, and they have to do something about it. Police stations aren't the place for mentally ill people in any event.

There is a protocol for this. If a person is taken off the street under the Mental Health Act, the NHS is duty-bound to make an assessment and deal with it. So off we go to our local hospital, which did have a mental health wing. I looked after the unfortunate man while my idiot colleague spoke to doctors. Completely against all protocol ever published, the doctor persuaded my colleague that the man should be taken to a police station. They felt that this hospital wasn't the best place for him and, inexplicably, the police station was. I said that I would have nothing to do with it. The police station was essentially being used as a place of safety and, where we had powers to remove a person *to* a place of safety, we had no powers to remove a person *from* one place of safety (the hospital in this case) to another – unless the first was clearly unsuitable. The day a hospital is deemed 'unsuitable' for someone who requires medical attention should be viewed as a bad day for the NHS. I was overruled but refused to have any hand in removing him.

He was taken back to the police station then put through the same process. But two doctors could not be found to declare him mentally ill. And now there was not a single hospital in the whole country who would accept him except for one in Dartmoor. This was on the condition that we took him there and stayed with him until he was assessed, then remove him if they decided he was mentally healthy. My bosses clearly told them to jog on. That would mean a 500-mile round journey for a driver, two other officers and a vehicle off the road for many hours. This left us with a problem. Someone with clear mental health issues, our duty to protect the public and the 72-hour clock running down rather rapidly. On the evening of the third day, we received a call at the station from our Superintendent. At his insistence, he had been kept abreast of the unfolding situation while off work. He informed us that we could not release the man, owing to the 'risk' he posed to the general public. We should, therefore, arrest him to 'prevent a breach of the peace' under common law. We could then keep him in custody for court in the morning. The arresting officer should not be concerned as he, the Superintendent, would be at court the following day as the officer in the case (OIC) therefore taking any flak that the court wanted to dish out. True to his word, he was at court, suited and booted the very next day. The officer who caused all this – my idiot colleague – was conspicuous by his absence at court. He, of course, got a flea in his ear for being had over by the NHS Doctors.

What happened to the unfortunate man? Nothing. There is only one sanction for people being brought before the court for breach of the peace. That is that they are 'bound over to keep the peace' for a set period. The court is allowed to do nothing more. So he was released. But at least it was by the court and not by the police. We were covered. As for the NHS, he wasn't in a hospital, so not their problem. And I'm not sure they could care less.

I don't like criticising the NHS, they do an excellent job most of the time. On this occasion, they signally failed at every level, ably assisted by my colleague... did I mention he was an idiot. It's worth mentioning in the meantime that my wife hates Ian Hislop, the editor of Private Eye. This is for no other reason than his resemblance to that idiot colleague. She, like myself, still cannot abide him, even now. We haven't seen or heard from him in over twenty years. Which is probably just as well. If being in possession of an offensive personality was an imprisonable offence, he'd be a lifer.

In terms of the rest of the Public Order Act, it is fairly straight forward and operates largely, albeit unusually, on common-sense. The least serious offence would be Section 5, which is about people causing problems for others trying to go about their business in public. The law states, that if the police come across this, they have to warn the aggressor of the behaviour that is causing the problem. If the person continues, they get arrested. Fortunately, the law is not prescriptive. I think the writers realised that disturbances are organic changing and developing at their own pace. As long as the officer is clear in his instructions, it doesn't matter what he says. So, "Oy! Cut that out or you'll be nicked!" is perfectly acceptable in the right circumstances. We also have specific legislation to deal with racially abusive public order, again this is reasonably sensible. The only issue I have ever come across with this, is having to deal with people who think that, just because they are of an ethnic minority themselves, the laws on racial abuse don't apply to them. Racial abuse is unnecessary and unpleasant in any setting regardless of the colour of your skin and whether or not you are on the receiving end or are dishing it out.

Drugs

This is a subject that is evolving in my mind all the time. Take away the prejudices and preconceived notions, start from the beginning and it all becomes a bit of a grey area. On the face of it, the subject is fairly straight forward: just say no! But some anomalies don't quite fit. I will be expounding in a later chapter on my views that the suppliers of illicit narcotics are considered a greater danger than the users, but you can't have one without the other. But for now, I will be asking how did we get to the stage of having either side? Well, I would suggest that it was created by governmental masterminds (Sorry, just have to drag my tongue from my cheek before continuing).

I'm not suggesting that there were a bunch of MPs in a darkened vault beneath the corridors of power, all laughing maniacally while deliberately creating drug users and suppliers in some weird test-tube experiment. I just suggest their utter incompetence and election fuelled tunnel vision was to blame.

Illegalisation

Let's take it from a time in the deep, distant, murky past when many of these narcotics were perfectly legal. Heroin is a trade name. It was devised in a lab and properly marketed. People were prescribed it for easing mental difficulties. Even soldiers were sent the stuff in goodie packages by their relatives. The problem was that the pharmaceutical companies - and the general medical profession - knew of its addictive properties. This was – and to some extent still is – a phenomenon rife in America. However, it was not a problem in the same way it is today. The pharmaceuticals essentially encouraged the medical profession to use it, conspicuously knowing that people would become addicted and, therefore assuring, a source income. The doctors were equally at fault, prescribing the drugs while being aware of the risk of addiction and failing to put any exit strategies in place for those who fell victim.

If we put politicians into the mix, you get chaos. What the politicians did – and the reader may notice some modern-day similarities in America with cocaine based products – was to recognise a growing problem and react with typical knee-jerk responses. What they did was to illegalise heroin. Just like that. So all those people who were using the stuff as prescribed by their GPs, had their legitimate supply cut off overnight. We are talking thousands of people. Many high-profile entertainers of the 40s and 50s, all needing a substance that was now suddenly illegal.

Such is the nature of addiction, these unfortunate people couldn't just stop. Obviously, pharmaceutical companies knew this. They had to stopped production, which allowed the industry to be taken over by the shadier sections of our society. By sending the whole thing underground, all the safety clauses that were put in place by the various trading standards agencies went out the window. There was no legislation to control the quality or the quantity of heroin. Street criminals then realised a little niche market and started buying the stuff and adding cheaper ingredients to increase their profit margins. It was these additives that made the drug the killer it is today.

Heroin was never a dangerous drug that caused people to die when used in the right proportions that were prescribed and regulated. It only became dangerous when it was being 'cut' with other substances, then sold by unqualified dealers to people who were addicted. It also became possible for these dealers to create their own market by causing the addictions in the first place. So, when people think of heroin as dangerous and likewise the users, just remember if this stuff was legalised, the doctors would be able to prescribe it. This would then be subject to a strict Code of Practice that would demand an exit strategy for the patients. The government would then be able to have control over quality. It would mean that these substances would not be as dangerous. Still addictive, but not dangerous. Of course, countries like Afghanistan, who make their living out of growing the poppy plants used to manufacture the substance, would then be legitimised and criminals would have to look elsewhere to spread their misery. I know this is a little idyllic, but I do believe that if the politicians hadn't caused this to happen in the first place, we wouldn't have the problems we see today.

So, do we really think that the suppliers were the real villains here? Were they not just taking advantage of political expedience? If they are the villains, then the pharmaceuticals are arch criminals, and the doctors their lackeys.

In this day and age, I have little sympathy for the users. This has been going on for a hundred years and we all know what the dangers are. We are all equally aware of the law surrounding it. I am aware that social deprivation and mental health and so on, are all factors, but every single person who uses heroin now has, at some point in their lives, taken a sober decision to use it with all this knowledge at their fingertips.

This theme runs throughout the entire world of illicit drugs. I personally have never used any form of illicit drug knowingly. It takes enough just to get me to take over-the-counter pharmaceuticals as it is, so illegal drugs aren't going to happen. Having said that, I don't live in a cave. I am a Londoner – if not by birth, then certainly by the fact that I have spent nearly three-quarters of my life living in the city. I am therefore acquainted with many social users of these substances. I am also acquainted with – and support – people who are developing and promoting the medical advantages of drugs like cannabis.

It makes my blood boil when I hear doctors and politicians tell us that they are "not sure about the medical advantages of cannabis" and that further tests are needed because "they just don't have enough information". This is baloney! They have done more tests on cannabis than you can shake a stick at. They know more about cannabis than any other substance, legal or otherwise.

When these people say, "We only have anecdotal evidence for that," all I hear is, 'cop-out!' When proper scientists hear those words, the very first thing that they should be thinking is, "no smoke without fire, let's do some experiments and find out." In this way, 'anecdotal' would become 'empirical' and there could be no argument.

My cynical side now wants to take over. I could suggest that they won't use the stuff on a medical footing because the pharmaceutical companies have not been able to corner this particular market – and the politicians are being lobbied to distraction by these companies to keep it out of legitimate suppliers' hands. I will try to resist the temptation to succumb to my cynical side and allow others to make up their own mind. In the meantime, of course, the pharmaceutical companies are working their fingers to the bone to limit production of cannabinoids to themselves and their buddies, while convincing the politicians that it isn't a viable product. At least until they have all their ducks in a row that is. Then it will be the 'new' elixir of life. 'New evidence suggests...' and all that gumph.

I am reminded of a TV programme that was distinctly anti-pharmaceutical (and therefore could do no wrong in my view). I have heard the whole thing described as a conspiracy theory... then again those who say this don't seem to understand the concept of conspiracy theories. It doesn't take much imagination to realise that these companies are private profit-making organisations. For example, say a company came up with two solutions to a specific medical condition. One would cure it outright for a relatively hefty price, and the other would deal with the symptoms only, thereby causing the patient to have to continue that medication over an extended period. Even if this medication was a fifth of the cost per dose, they would still secure a profit. I do not believe that pharmaceutical companies have any interest in curing anything. They wouldn't make money that way. I am not a fan of putting businesses into public hands. If you want to cure the world's diseases, the best way is to remove profit margins bearing in mind the above issues, and a good start is to nationalise. It isn't like the expense would be prohibitive. From a long term perspective, it would be comparatively cheaper.

Anyway, this programme. It has been a long time since I watched it and I can't remember what it was called, but there are many websites like Food Matters that support what was said. They expounded on the idea that vitamins had strong medicinal properties, and that pharmaceutical companies were playing the science down. We have all heard of the idea that we can theoretically overdose on vitamins. So they decided to experiment on this. There was a theory that vitamin-C could assist in the control of blood cancers. They had an idea of what the recommended daily allowance (RDA) of the vitamin was, so they used that as a base. They increased the doses in a hundred patients gradually and eventually went as high as 250-times the RDA, which they injected directly into the blood vessels. They found out two surprising things. Firstly, in 90% of cases, the disease stopped advancing, and in some cases, actually retreated. Secondly, in 100% of cases, there were no adverse reactions. These are unprecedented figures.

Pharmaceuticals will tell you that there are at least a dozen recorded cases where an overdose of vitamins may have contributed to a death in the past decade. In the meantime, according to the documentary, hundreds of thousands of deaths every single year occur as a direct, proven result of correctly prescribed, correctly administered pharma. So why aren't the scientists advancing this tech? Could it just be the fact that they can't copyright vitamin-C? And they certainly wouldn't be able to make profits from this alone. Oh, that cynical voice just keeps coming back.

Cannabis

Didn't we have fun with the legislation surrounding cannabis? How can something so simple be made so difficult? So, cannabis was always a Class B drug. In the world of classifications, Class A is addictive and illegal to possess in any form, for any reason. Class B is less addictive but is also psychoactive. It's illegal to have possession of it in any form for any reason. Class C is prescription only, everything else is over the counter with few if any controls. So, cannabis is illegal to possess. It isn't illegal to use. There is no legislation dealing with that. Just possession. You can't own it, grow it or keep it on behalf of someone else. And I think you may have difficulty in using it without possessing it. Many politicians wanted to legalise it. Some, because they wanted to use it, some because they didn't want to spend money policing it, and some just wanted to show a crime reduction. Take out a whole piece of legislation and you take away a whole bunch of recorded crime. It would then show that you have reduced crime. Heroic! Hurray! And back to the office for tea and medals!

How do you legalise something like this? I started smoking cigarettes in the early 70s. I was aware that even then, they were commonly referred to as 'cancer sticks' or 'coffin nails'. I also know that this was the case in the 60s and possibly even as early as the late 50s. Despite that, there are people today trying to take the tobacco industry to court because "they are to blame for my addiction. I would never have started If I had known that cigarettes were unhealthy" and so on. Yeah, right! A distinct odour of bovine excrement here. But this makes a difference. The sort of cannabis that's available on the illegal market today, is much stronger than the stuff they were using in the '60s. It is causing a lot of mental health complications, especially in younger users. This is not just my opinion; you only need to ask any mental health nurse just how many young people they are dealing with in their hospitals that have been diagnosed with drug-induced psychoses. So the government won't legalise it because in 50 years' time people will be taking the producers – or worse, the government – to court for allowing them to use a substance that was directly responsible for their mental issues. And can you give me many millions of pounds in compensation so that I don't have to work ever again, and can remain stoned for the rest of my life? Never mind that they are absolutely aware of the dangers right now. So they couldn't just legalise it.

Their solution was to make it a Class-C and then ensure that medical professionals didn't prescribe it. This, they thought, was a cunning plan. They didn't consider that young people are, by and large, stupid. Regardless of how loudly you shouted it from the rooftops, the youngsters just thought that 'Class-C' meant it was legal. The suppliers rubbed their collective hands together because they could see demand increasing and nowhere to get the stuff legally. So, illegal possession went through the roof. It wasn't prosecuted much, but it had to be recorded when it came to police attention. The 'cunning plan' was not quite so cunning as was first they thought. The solution? Reverted back to Class B as the current situation was sending mixed messages.

I think the stuff is now, to all intents and purposes, legal. The establishment stick their fingers in their ears and say "La, la, la, la," every time they hear the word drug. They will tell the entire world that they never legalised it when someone tries to prosecute but ignore it until that day. In the meantime, there are people out there who would benefit from the medical wonders that the CBD and THC oils that are extracted from the cannabis plant, but they can't get access to it because of political intransigence. I believe the legislation is in place for the medical profession to legally prescribe CBD oil, and they are still deciding on THCs. The professionals are still reluctant to prescribe it. It seems they would rather dish out some chemically produced pharma over this natural product.

To make a comparison, cocaine-based products are not so clear cut. America is in the grip of an addiction epidemic caused by the over-prescription of codeine, co-codamol, and the like. When paired with ongoing undermanagement of the consequences, it seems that they refuse to learn from even recent history. Either that or their greed takes the front seat. Watch this space, is all I'll say.

This brings me to an anecdote. It does not illustrate the above point. It is merely a mildly humorous 'what if' scenario.

We were called to the scene of an ongoing burglary. Apparently, a nosey neighbour had spotted our old pal Billy Burglar loading a TV into the back of a Trannie (that is to say Transit van, not 'person with alternative sexual preferences'). The Neighbour had obviously spotted the fact that Billy looked somewhat shady, so he looked further down the road. From his vantage point, he could see a door hanging off its hinges and put two and two together. Police turn up and Billy gets the benefit of free bed and board for a few hours. We go to the scene of the crime. As we go in, the stench of cannabis is overpowering. You could almost cut the air with a knife. A little sleuthing discovers that the loft has had a small cannabis growing enterprise. The cannabis had been harvested, and the results were in two rather large bin bags in the kitchen.

It didn't come as a complete shock that the occupant didn't come forward and Billy's character was not further besmirched. But here is the thing... had Billy got away with it, he would have got £50 for the TV. Had he been prosecuted, maybe a few weeks at HM's pleasure. As it happened, he both got caught *and* wasn't prosecuted. So, the whole thing was for nothing on all sides. What if Billy had a second brain cell to keep his other one company and had spotted the large bin liners? Our nosey neighbour would only have seen Billy walking down the road with an innocuous bin liner, and probably would have thought nothing of it. He would not have looked down the road and would not have noticed the break-in. If Billy is caught, he could claim that he didn't know what was in the bag. He had just nicked it and was going to have a butcher's in a safer place. The amount of cannabis in the bag would have attracted a charge of possession with intent to supply. But Billy didn't know what was in the bag. So how can he form an intention about what to do with the contents? The police may have a charge of possession of Class B. He wouldn't have endured any kind of custodial for that. Let's be honest, the occupant is never going to write a loser's statement for that amount of cannabis. He would be lining himself up for a supplying charge. If, of course, Billy does get away with it – which seems more likely – no one will be calling the police, so no burglary would be recorded or investigated. He would then have a couple of grands worth of weed at his disposal. Just saying. The way it ended up, the police got to destroy a shed load of cannabis, the TV would have been sold at auction, the occupant would have lost both. Billy would have gained nothing but a free lunch.

Interviews

One of the skill areas that is often overlooked is interviewing. When it comes to interviewing people for jobs and such like, the interviewer is trying to find out about the interviewee; what the person is like; how they think, what they'd be like in the work environment, and so on. The interviewers usually have a list of boxes to tick every time the person being grilled hits a mark. The more ticks, the better. It sounds all nice a fair. All down the line and devoid of anything discriminatory. Of course, we are talking about people here, there will always be an element of subjectivity. Interviewing people about specific moments in time – which is what police do – is an entirely different type of skill. The best ones can walk away from an interview having extracted every minute detail of a moment in time. The ones with a lower skill set will walk away with only the information they set out to obtain.

Once again, our beloved media – in the form of TV police dramas – give a false impression of what happens in any interview. The lawyer that sits with their client, for example, is absolutely not allowed to answer questions on behalf of their client. I was never interested in what advice the solicitor had to offer me. He was there to advise his client, not me. I did, however, have good working relationships with most solicitors. We were both professionals doing our jobs, but there were boundaries. When it came to it, the interview room was most definitely my domain.

In fact, a solicitor had little effect on what questions would be asked, as well as how they would be asked. If you think about it, the whole purpose of conducting an interview is to try to obtain information to further an investigation. The information that you are trying to extract isn't going to change by the mere presence of a solicitor, so naturally, neither would the questions. What generally happens is that a solicitor is called at the request of the detainee. The representative is given a brief overview of the case. The detainee is then allowed to have a private consultation before the interview commences. From here, the solicitor usually remains entirely silent, save to "remind their client of their previous advice". That's it. Sometimes they'll ask for – and be granted – a further private consultation, but beyond that, they do very little. They certainly wouldn't have any affected any decision regarding the investigation, and whether or not their client is charged, bailed or otherwise.

As a general rule, I was happy to have solicitors in the interviews. It gave them less of an argument when it came to redacting elements of the interview for the purposes of court proceedings. What I didn't like, was that the solicitor's consultation was done while the custodial clock was ticking. If they decided that they were going to have a 5-hour consultation, I could do nothing about it. This meant that any opportunity to investigate disclosures while the person was still in custody was reduced. There was one occasion when, for reasons that I can't remember, the 24-hour limit (that is the time police are allowed to detain anyone without charge) was rapidly approaching. We had all of 5 hours remaining and the person hadn't been interviewed. We called his solicitor in, briefed him and allowed them their consultation. This usually takes between 30 minutes and an hour, depending on how complex the investigation was. There was, of course, no actual limit on how long they were allowed to take. On this occasion, I believe quite deliberately, the solicitor was in consultation for 4 and a half hours. He thought that it would leave me a very short period of time to interview his client. Hoping that this would mean the interview would not be thorough. In the event, I approached a senior officer who had the power to extend the custody time by up to 12 hours provided the reasons were sound and the purpose was lawful. On that occasion, I explained what actions we had taken in the previous 19 hours and provided a reasonable explanation for the interview being conducted at such a late stage. He took the same view as me. His time was extended by 2 hours, which was more than adequate for my purposes. The smug look on the solicitor's face was wiped off when he was told. Essentially, he had already informed me that his consultation was complete. I then invited the senior officer to explain the decision. The solicitor could not then reasonably go back into another 2-hour consultation. I conducted the interview, happy in the knowledge that I had plenty of time to extract what information I needed. The solicitor was spitting feathers as he left. He was clearly one of the few who thought that it was a battle against the police every time. It wasn't. It never was. He was an idiot.

I've said it before, and I'll say it again. There are three basic scenarios in all interviews. Obviously, there are variations – some of which will overlap. However, the three most apparent are either, "I wasn't there, I don't know what you're talking about", "I was there, but I didn't do it. It was someone else", or "I was there, and I did the deed"

I would say, if you fall into the latter of the three, you're better off making no comment to all questions. Let the investigator prove it, you have nothing to lose and everything to gain by your silence. You don't need a solicitor for that. All that would happen if you asked for a solicitor is that you would end up spending longer in custody while you awaited the arrival of the solicitor. We don't keep a box of them in a cupboard ready and waiting. They have to be called in.

If you fall into the first category, I would be shouting it from the rooftops. You have everything to lose and nothing to gain in silence. If you weren't there, then you should be able to prove it. There is little logic in putting yourself through a load of trouble for no reason. This would simply mean telling the truth. You don't need solicitor's advice for that. All that would happen is that you end up spending longer in custody while you awaited the arrival of the solicitor.

If you fall into the middle category, it may get a little more complicated. It would mean that you could be pointing the finger at someone else. Obviously, if it were me and someone else was responsible for doing something, there is no way I would take the fall for it. You do the crime; you do the time. Simple. Others may have other issues which make it difficult for them to do that.

Along with the three different basic scenarios, there are three basic ways an interview will go. These more or less include answering no questions (as is your right), answering all questions put to you or providing a prepared statement before reverting to one of the first two options.

As I said earlier, everyone wants to be believed unquestioningly, but consider how often you hear something like, "I was never there, I was 200 miles away in Manchester at the time. My bank statement will show that and CCTV can prove it." So even though people want to be believed, they will always look to corroborate where they can.

If you are going to tell porkies in an interview, be very careful. Remembering an incident is a basic function of your brain. People do remember things slightly differently, but there will always be a consistent thread. All you are doing is extracting something that exists as an event within your memory. When you lie, you have to use a different part of the brain - your imagination. Then you have to remember what you have said in the right order. Catching someone out lying is not difficult, and it is the same process as getting the truth out. Ask lots of questions. Come at it from different angles. Fine detail is great. If you are telling the truth, it will always come out the same. You have to be an accomplished liar to maintain the lie under skilful interrogation.

When I interviewed, I seldom challenged an account if I knew it was a lie. My strategy was to continue to develop a story until the interviewee was so entrenched, they couldn't get out of it. Often this meant stopping the interview after I had drained them of all the information they had. I would then go over the account with a fine-toothed comb, pick out the inconsistencies, and all the information that contradicted known facts. I would then return to the 'challenge' phase. I did this once in an interview that was being conducted by a colleague. The interviewee was obviously and clearly lying through his back teeth. We knew this. My colleague was just about to launch into the interviewee with what he thought would have been a devastating rebuttal of everything he had said when I interjected and called the interview to a close. This allowed me to consult with my colleague in private. If the interviewee can do it, why not me? My colleague was a little put out for having the wind taken out of his sails. When I sat him down and went through the interview, the penny dropped. We came up with 20 areas that we could challenge him on. Most of which would have been overlooked had we not taken a time-out.

It was a strange interview. It started with the interviewee saying, "no comment." To everything. As we were closing the interview, my colleague said. "Is there anything you want to tell us before we conclude? It may be your last chance." He then launched into a half-an-hour long tale of woe. He just went on and on. We couldn't stop him. The old adage, 'if you find yourself in a hole, stop digging' never occurred to him. He did think he lived on a higher intellectual plane than we did and would be able to counter any argument we put forward. You can't argue the facts. He tried... and he failed.

I have had them all. I once had a man who wouldn't stop talking until I turned the recorder on. He then did not whisper a single syllable throughout the interview. Not even a name. Not even a fart or burp, nothing. I then turned the recorder off. The moment I did this, he turned back on. There was only the interviewee and me in the interview room. If you were to hear it, you would only hear one person in the room, me. He knew the score. This was a domestic assault. He would get charged and would go to court the next day. She would not show up because 'he said he was sorry and he would never do it again' for the fiftieth time. Because she didn't show, there would be no evidence and he would be acquitted. And repeat. I once had two interviews in two days. Two completely separate investigations where the first words to come out of both interviewees was, "I'm sorry I lied in the previous interview..." It took the wind right out of my sails. One continued with a different set of lies, the other came out with the truth.

In the end, interviews are not worth much in a legal sense. The interviewee can change his account almost at will with very little in the way of consequences. TV dramas will have you believe that the police want you to admit all. Confession is everything. As long as you have that, your case is solved, closed and everyone goes off to the pub for beers and medals. Admissions are not worth the paper they are written on without substantial corroboration. I would get more out of a pack of lies than I would ever get out of an admission. Solicitors would rip any admission evidence up in court without a second glance. So no, confessions aren't any use in anything other than TV cop dramas.

We must always be aware that solicitors and barristers aren't interested in the truth. They cannot advise you to lie. They cannot defend a 'not guilty' plea for someone who has admitted their guilt. Their consultation is absolutely private, and they will not disclose anything said. However, they are duty-bound to step down and claim something that the legal profession like to call being 'professionally embarrassed' if they become aware that their client is lying. This can't be policed in any way, because no one ever gets to know what is said in consultation. This means we have to rely on the honesty of the legal adviser. If they are not actually told that their client is guilty, they are blissful in their ignorance and will carry on regardless. I actually overheard a barrister talking to a colleague saying that he was about to go into trial. He had two defences that he could use and wondered which one he would go for. The truth, perhaps? That might be helpful. What am I saying?! This is a court of law. It's about guilty or not guilty – not truth and lies. They aren't in the slightest bit interested in that. It's all about the academic process. Defendants and witnesses are an unfortunate necessity.

It is my sad experience that if a defendant spends his entire time in the evidential box, telling lie after lie but then slots in one morsel of truth, this truth becomes everything to the case. The defendant must be as honest as the day is long. If a witness is truthful throughout but is caught out in one single lie, everything that came before must, by extension, be a tissue of lies regardless of evidential matters.

I have so far given the law and its practitioners a hard time. Here's an example of when those on the receiving end – the defendants – are their own worst enemies. It is a case that I dealt with, which involved five suspects in a 'stranger rape' case. This entailed at least three of them putting a young woman through an ordeal the like of which I would never wish on anyone. The suspects were identified through CCTV and Oyster card records. One of the few times that CCTV has been pivotal in identifying suspects. The first of the suspects came to the police station of his own volition when he heard that he was being sought by police. He claimed to speak only Dutch and Swahili, and the latter was not great. It was a lie. He was close friends with the other four. None of them spoke anything other than English. He obviously thought he was inconveniencing me. He didn't seem to understand that I was being paid to be there, he wasn't, so it was his time that he was wasting. We got a Dutch interpreter eventually. You won't believe how difficult that is. The Dutch are great linguists, and I have never come across any who didn't have a good grasp of the English language. This results in Dutch interpreters being few and far between because they are just not needed. He was eventually interviewed. He admitted being there but denied any knowledge of the event as he 'left early'. I believe he was the mover-and-shaker but didn't do the deed. He was about 20 at the time – a little older than all the others who were teenagers. The other four were arrested, interviewed and then released on bail. One denied all knowledge (and I believed him – I think he got scared and walked away before anything happened). One claimed consent, one gave a story that implicated the fifth person, and the fifth person made 'no comment' to all questions put. The investigation continued, and they were all invited back for a further interview to challenge their accounts. The first two stated that their initial account was truthful, and would not add anything further. 'No comment' to all questions put. The third confirmed his initial statement, saying the girl provided oral sex consensually. He then stated that he left her with the other two. Number four continued to blame number five and number five made 'no comment'. So, number five could not be placed at the scene, but all the others put themselves there.

A fingertip search had been conducted at the scene of the crime. This was a public recreation ground, but fortunately, it had been sealed off in the early hours and was undisturbed. A condom wrapper matching what the victim had described was found and a fingerprint was lifted. This matched the fingerprints of Mr 'No comment', thereby placing him on the scene nice and neatly. He was re-interviewed and, somewhat unsurprisingly no comment was made.

Now, this is where it gets interesting. Three were eventually charged and went to Crown Court. The prosecution case was put and all the suspect interviews – 14 in total – were played to the jury. The one who admitted having sex stuck to his story, and stated it was all consensual but inexplicably left her alone with the other two once he had fulfilled his needs. The one who blamed number five refused to take the stand, giving no evidence in court and relying on his interview that blamed the other boy. Number five came on and pointed his accusing finger at number four, claiming that he did the deed.

In these cases, the judge can direct a jury to 'draw their own conclusions' when someone does not answer any questions during the investigation but chooses to provide one for the jury. They can also be directed in similar terms when the defendant does provide an account to police but refuses to give evidence in court. They can also be directed to consider the strength of evidence when the defendants start accusing each other, usually in an effort to get themselves out of the hole they have just dug. This, rather delightfully, is known as a 'cut-throat' defence in the legal sphere. It was quite entertaining to sit back and watch them convict themselves, particularly in the knowledge of what they had put this poor victim through.

Written Statements

Not all interviews are for suspects. Some are victim or witness interviews. This is usually done on a form that includes a 'statement of truth' that has to be signed, telling the world that you aren't lying, promise, cross my heart and hope to die. This statement has a space for your name and a place to sign it. So before you got to the actual writing. You had identified yourself and signed a declaration.

When I was at detective training school, which was in the same complex as the recruit training facility, the investigative experts, (by which I mean the guys training the detectives), had a basic structure of the statement. It would start something like,

"This statement describes the circumstances surrounding the break-in to my home and the theft of my property. I am the owner and occupier of (insert address) and the owner of all the property that was kept within." It will then go on to describe what happened from the witness's point of view. The next section would go on to describe any suspects. The next paragraph would be to list the property.

The people training the recruits decided that they were the experts and would have a different way of dealing with it. They felt that the structure should be more rigid and start with the phrase, "I am the above-named person, and I live at an address known to police." This was always nonsense, who else would "I" be? Would there be an occasion where it would start, "I am not actually the above-named person, but I thought I'd have my say anyway"? In addition to that, if it is about the burglary of your home or the address was an integral part of the incident, then the address is a vital piece of evidence and it has to go in. If the statement is about something where your address has no bearing, simply don't mention it. Again, would there be an occasion where you'd be saying,"... and I will be staying somewhere the police will never find me"? No, probably not. Not as a witness or victim at least, but the trainers couldn't be told. What would then follow was something that had little structure and would often lead trainees to forget certain pivotal things – like the address of the incident. So, what then happened is that we had to unteach this nonsense when the recruits were released into the big wide world. Of course, too many recruits were coming through and we couldn't catch up, so now we have quite senior people thinking that this is the only way to start and complete a statement. If a uniformed officer offered to take a statement from a witness, I would sometimes – if the case was serious enough – tell them not to worry and that I would do it.

I found it quite amusing that officers would invest a lot of time ensuring that a victim or witness address was not revealed in any way in any paperwork, only to write out an arrest note that included the address of the victim or witness. You'd get officers making sure the address doesn't appear in the statements of any witness, or the crime report. Any paperwork peripheral to the incident would then be redacted, and they would write in their arrest report something akin to, "On [insert date and time] I attended [insert address] where I spoke to the victim of a theft... the victim named the suspect and told me where he would be found and I attended that address..." It is quite legitimate to withhold an address to protect witnesses but that means not mentioning it anywhere. We could redact the offending lines without any real problem, but it doesn't look great to the jury when there are gaps or blacked-out areas of a written statement

The Caution

As a final sideswipe at the system, I am covering the phenomenon of cautioning. It is mentioned later on in terms of human rights, but right now, I will deal with the mechanics.

Up until the 1990s, anyone who was going to be questioned by police where their answers could incriminate them had to be cautioned. This was in the terms, "You do not have to say anything, but anything you do say may be given in evidence."

It is used in very limited circumstances now, but at the time, that is what you got. A load of boffins at educational facilities around the country decided that some of the most intelligent people in the country would not understand the full impact of this short, simple sentence on first hearing it. So, what do the politicians do? They complicate it, of course.

It was correctly believed that people would take their rights to silence and not answer questions. They would then go home and get together with their mates working out a story that they could put to the court. When it came to the hearing, a perfectly dovetailed alibi was ready and waiting with witnesses queuing up to take the stand in strict chronological order. Police could do nothing about it as they would not have heard it until that point. Occasionally, the investigation was very thorough and managed to deal with whatever they were saying, but often by pure chance. It was unusual for police to disprove alibi evidence so people got off with some quite serious offences because they could.

"We can't have this!" says our political elite, so we end up with the following caution:

'You do not have to say anything, but it may harm your defence if you do not mention when questioned something that you later rely on in court, anything you do say may be given in evidence'

So, if the first one was too complex for the most intelligent people, what chance did the majority of the people who heard the new caution for the first time have? Because ultimately, most of them were not intelligent. If they were, they wouldn't be criminals. Well, not the sort that got themselves caught, anyway. We always explained the caution in layman's terms, but I often felt that it just wasn't sinking in. It is not particularly difficult – if you don't answer my questions now and try it on with the jury, the jury can reject what you say if they want. If what you have to say to the jury is true, it would have been so when you were first interviewed, fresher in your memory, and would have been more impactive.

Identification Issues

An area in which the law is east, reality is west, and ne'er the twain shall meet. This is an area of law that has been designed by lawyers for lawyers.

It seems to me that whatever police do in this area, they will get it wrong. If they comply with everything, the defence is given too many ways of destroying the evidence. If they don't, the defence will claim that the identification is flawed and the whole case is therefore unsafe.

Here is a hypothetical scenario for you to grapple with to demonstrate the process.

Someone approaches the police and makes an allegation. We will use the allegation of assault to keep it simple. They state that it happened 5 minutes previously, and they went off in 'that' direction. A description is given to police which is then recorded. The officers notice that there are open wounds to the victim.

From here, several different things can happen:

A police officer in the area spots what appears to be a pair that closely match the recorded descriptions. In approaching them, the officer notices what seems to be blood spatters on their clothing. They are unresponsive to questions and appear to have injuries on their knuckles. In this case, the police must ensure that the victim and suspects do not come into contact with each other. The suspects are then whisked away and formal *ID procedures are initiated*

If we use the same scenario with the same police officer and the same suspects. In this case, however, there is no evidence of blood or any signs of aggression. The descriptions were a little generic, so the officer cannot be certain that these are the aggressors. In this case, the victim should be taken for a 'drive around'. The suspects should be in the presence of plain-clothed officers where possible. The victim cannot be led in any way. Uniformed officers holding neon-lit arrows pointing directly at the suspect is not considered very sporting. Police can point in the general direction of groups of people, but recognition has to come from the victim alone. If the victim can't identify the suspects, then further investigation should be carried out. If further evidence comes to light, then action can be taken appropriate to that information. If they are identified, the victim must be kept away from any further contact at all costs, and the suspect arrested so that formal *ID procedures are initiated.*

I the event that there are no suspects initially apparent to the officers, then the victim can be shown a series of photographs. There has to be 12 or more photographs of different individuals. Why 12, I cannot say, but then, the whole reason for me writing this is that I can't figure out what is going on in the law-makers' heads. If the police have a suspect in mind, the photo of that person can be put into the album, but nothing should be done to make this obvious. If someone is identified – which is a rare thing indeed – the suspect is traced, investigated, and if they can be placed in the area at the time, formal *id procedures are initiated.*

Now, it used to be that police would line up eight people. They would then ask the victim to walk up to them and point out whodunnit. They couldn't put a 16-year-old skinny white youth in a line-up of eight 60+ black grannies. That was another tactic that wasn't considered 'good sport'. Police had to make an effort to make everyone in the line-up look similar. These days it's all changed. Some 'bright spark' has decided that identification has to be facial only. So, if you hobble into a bank on crutches with only one leg, you also have one blind eye and a tattoo on your right arm saying, 'I am a bank robber'. If you are wearing a face covering and the witnesses can't see your face, ID is out the window. You may be able to get those physical traits into evidence but not through ID procedures. All ID is now done on video. A video recording of the suspect is taken, showing head and shoulders. The subject has to be recorded looking left, right and straight ahead. So the concept of build, height or any other non-facial trait is ignored. A load of other archived videos of similar looking people, who have freely given their image for this purpose, are retrieved from the computer. Eight separate videos, each with the same eight people – including the suspect in each one – are edited to show each individual in random places. The witness is then asked to choose one disk which is then viewed, and an identification is made... or not.

It must be said at this point that the defence will almost always challenge any of this evidence. If the person was identified on the street first, the defence can argue that the initial ID was faulty, and the victim is just picking out the person he saw in the street – who was an innocent passer-by. Mug shots will often elicit a similar response, The defence team will say that it wasn't their client and the victim is merely identifying the person in the mug shot, not the guy who assaulted him.

Even if someone was to approach a police officer, having been assaulted by a stranger the previous day, and points the suspect out to the officer there and says, "that guy over there is the geezer wotdunnit." ID procedures still have to be initiated with the same get-out that the solicitors always have. If any of these procedures are not complied with to the letter, the prosecution risk having the entire procedure excluded.

We now have an entire industry built around this procedure. There are offices – called ID suites – dotted around London, staffed by civilian staff, Constables, Sergeants and Inspectors whose only job is to complete ID procedures.

Having delved into the ways in which ID procedures are initiated and carried out, I now want to demonstrate to you how painstakingly complicated – and ultimately frustrating –they can and have been in practice.

My first example is a nasty racially aggravated GBH on an Asian man by a group of mixed-race youths. The victim believed the assailants to be local and even had an idea of one of their names. For the purposes of anonymity, let's say that name was Adam. Now it gets a little complicated here. All the following happens over the course of several weeks. One of the lads is arrested and admits being part of the attack. He is, of course, charged. A second is arrested soon after. It quickly becomes evident that there is mounting evidence showing that he was not involved in the assault. In this case, formal *ID procedures are initiated*. The victim was then shown mugshots to try to identify the other assailants. At this point, something very rare occurred. They identified someone, and that someone was the aforementioned 'Adam'. He lived locally and had a somewhat fitting reputation when concerning the accusation at hand. Even more promising – one might hope – is that he was a known associate of the other two. Formal *ID procedures are initiated*. Before continuing, it should be borne in mind that the mugshots are dealt with and shown to the witness by an officer with no knowledge of the case, nor the investigation surrounding it. Therefore, we can eliminate any chance of encouragement on the part of the investigating body as to which images to pick out.

I ten took the victim to complete the ID procedure for the second detainee (the one where I thought that there was mounting evidence that, although he was associated with the other lads, he wasn't involved in the assault). As anticipated, the person is not identified. I drove the victim home after the viewing and, as we are approaching his road, he points to a youth who is walking away from us and says, 'that's the boy, Adam. That's him.' I continue driving passed the man. I was able to make out that the passer-by was the individual picked out of the mug shots. Adam. I dropped the victim at his home and prepared a statement about what he had said to me. The investigation continued.

A week later, the first boy who was arrested went to court. The victim was required to attend. I met him outside the court and we waited for our case to be called. As we were sitting there, who should show up to provide support for his buddy? You guessed it, Adam. The victim once again spotted him and told me so. Another statement is taken. So, that is now three separate, random and unsolicited identifications on the same boy. I now have a problem. The formal ID procedures that have been started are in tatters on the floor. The victim has seen him three times, completely randomly. This would undoubtedly be used by the defence, and any attempt at using that evidence would be thrown out straight away. The principle that the victim and suspect should be kept separate throughout the ID procedure has clearly failed. There was no fault on anyone's part, but the defence would claim that any identification would be tainted because of this. I am aware of this, so I contact my local ID Suite and tell the Inspector in charge what has happened. It is agreed that the procedure should be abandoned. However, I, much like any other sensible person, didn't see ID as an issue. The victim knows Adam to look at, that much is obvious. So he's charged and goes to court. The court then threw the entire case out on the basis that the ID was 'unreliable'. Why? Because the formal ID procedures were not carried through. How wrong can you get that?

This next example is a little weird but, when you are beaten, sometimes its better to put your hands up. This was early in my career. I had never had anything to do with this side of the job. My role was purely peripheral, but it gave me an insight. One thing the law lords enacted to help the process was to require anyone going through these procedures not to change their appearance in a substantial way while the ID process was being conducted. If they did, the jury would be told, and the judge could then direct them that they could draw any adverse inferences that they deemed appropriate.

On this occasion, I was a uniformed officer tasked with taking a suspect from prison, where he had been contemplating his naval for several weeks, to the ID suite so that ID procedures could be completed. It was in the age of the old Line-up format. Several things were not really going in his favour. One was the fact that the victim was a portrait artist, and, had an above-average ability in recognising facial features. Another thing was that he had distinctive features. On the morning of the ID parade, the accused went to the prison barber and asked for a very specific haircut. He wanted the front half of his head clean-shaven and the back left as it was. On the way to the suite, I spoke to him about his hairdo. We chuckled about how ridiculous he looked. He was hoping that police wouldn't be able to find anyone who looked anything like that and therefore we'd have to abandon the whole procedure. Much – I'm sure – to his disdain, it ended up that all participants in the ID procedure were made to wear similar hats. He went to the lengths of looking rather stupid for nought, and the victim then had no trouble picking him from the line-up anyway. On the way back, he was still bullish as he thought that his solicitors would get the ID binned at court. In any event, the jury were left with the impression that he was trying to disguise himself. That is, of course, never going to go down very well.

The underlying problem with this whole subject is that no one seems to think it's about trying to get the identification right. No one seems to care whether a person has or has not done something. It is purely an academic exercise they can use to bash their substantial brains together over.

We don't recognise people purely on facial features. Ask yourself how many times you have walked into your office, or another place of work and a colleague is in the room facing away from you. Do you have to go right up to them and get them to turn and face you before you know who it is? I think not. Even people I know quite well in passing can be identifiable from behind. We use many different tools to identify people, voice; height; weight; the way someone walks or the set of their shoulders. Facial features are the icing on the cake but not the full story.

Forensics

Very misunderstood. Not just the word but the whole area and all the mysticism that surrounds it. Believe it or not, there is a world of difference between the word 'forensic' and the word 'forensics'. This is just one of a whole list of reasons that the word, as well as the whole area, is shrouded in mysticism and misunderstanding.

Let me explain. Most people, when asked what they thought the word 'forensic' meant, would tell me it is to do with fingerprints and DNA, and the science around that area of policing. Wrong! The word is derived from the Latin word 'forum'. A forum was where the city elders in Roman times would discuss issues of the day, complaints by the population, and generally, 'troubleshoot'. It was the forerunner to the modern-day courtroom. So, the meaning of forensic in modern parlance is, 'for and on behalf of the court.' What this means in practice, is that everything a police officer does in the course of his duty should be forensic. Everything police do has a possibility of being tested in court, and so it should be treated as such.

When police stations first started employing civilians to staff the front counters in an effort to free up warranted officers to roam the streets, they restricted what these employees could do. They felt that some tasks that had to be carried out by the people doing this job, were likely to be tested in court. Because of this, they wanted police officers to deal with those issues only. What they didn't realise was that everything that was ever put on paper was evidential. So if they were to take that to its logical conclusion, no civilian members-of-staff would have been allowed anywhere near a pen. Of course, that didn't happen. They would have been pointless. So they kind of brushed over that.

The meaning of 'forensics' on the other hand is an abbreviation of 'forensic science.' This is generally the sort of stuff used in court – fingerprint and DNA evidence, toxicology and so on. You will often hear archaeologists telling the world that they will carry out a 'forensic' search. By this, all they mean is a careful and thorough search, one that would never be subject to any court proceedings but was nevertheless painstaking. So common usage diminishes the word somewhat, but it still means 'for and on behalf of the court'.

So, there you have it. A statement that a police officer takes from a witness is a forensic statement. The language that legal eagles use in court is 'forensic language'. If the statement is about a forensic science issue, then it is a forensic statement about forensics. I'm glad that's cleared that up.

This chapter deals with forensics. We have all seen or heard of the TV dramas CSI Miami, silent witness, and the like. These give an unrealistic view of the weight that forensics can add to an investigation. Don't get me wrong, it is an important strand. However, it doesn't provide answers, only directions. All fingerprint or DNA evidence ever did was to tell the world that an individual had been in a particular place at some point prior to the sample being taken. It was always for the investigator to put the meat on the bones and prove that that person was there at a specific time for nefarious reasons. Something that DNA could never do. As we used to say in the Sexual Offences Department, "There is no 'Rape' DNA". The presence of DNA in intimate samples from a rape victim says that you did the deed. It doesn't say whether or not that deed was consented to.

If a woman alleges rape and, undergoes an intimate examination where DNA from a man is extracted, police would never go straight out and drag the bloke in, kicking and screaming, without conducting an investigation. She may well have had sexual congress, consensually with a man the day before. It would hardly be fair if it was that man who was identified and dragged in. Similarly, if we find our old friend Harry Housebreaker's fingerprints at the scene of a burglary, we have to make sure that the occupants don't know the guy. They could have had him around for cocktails and cucumber sandwiches on the portico the previous evening, we just don't know. If they have, then the evidence is useless. Unless, of course, the prints are found in an area where he wasn't allowed.

There was once an incident that was quite worrying, and never really resolved to my satisfaction. Once upon a time, a long time ago, there was a skinny runt of a drug-addicted white London youth. One day, he decided to go into a shop, threaten the owner, and steal the contents of the till. Because he was stupid (we thought), he left behind DNA at the scene. Later that day a knight in shining armour came riding to the rescue. This might be a slight exaggeration… he wasn't overly shiny, nor had been a knight of the realm. In fact, he was in a dark blue uniform with a silly pointy hat. The scene was examined, and a DNA profile extracted from samples taken from the scene. A statement was taken detailing the suspect's description. No matches were made immediately, so the DNA profile and case papers were kept on file. A year later, a 45-year-old, fat, East European bloke was trying his luck with the local damsels with varying degrees of success in a pub 5 miles from the scene. While he was regaling one such damsel with his tales of derring-do, he was approached by another man who did not have the eye for the local women. Oh no, he had set his sights on an entirely different sexual conquest. Unfortunately for him, his methods were a little too forward for our 45-year-old. In fact, he took offence at the sexual assault and, in an attempt to explain to the guy that he was, in fact, heterosexual, rearranged his facial features. Our man was duly arrested for assault, and a DNA sample was extracted as is the procedure in all cases.

The DNA was compared to those on file for unsolved cases. The assaulter was matched with the DNA from the till snatch. Now, the more observant of you will notice a slight difference in the features of the two men. I certainly spotted it when I went down to deal with the man in custody. It was so obviously not the skinny runt of a drug-addicted white London youth as previously described. Yet, the DNA sample was an exact match. He was clearly a man of previous good character before his little contretemps. He certainly wasn't a thief.

I called the scientists who basically said, if his DNA matches, he is your man whether you like it or not! Could we have mixed up the samples? Don't be ridiculous, we are scientists, we don't make mistakes! No change there then.

The man was clearly very concerned, no doubt with hundreds of thoughts going through his head. What if this youth killed someone? Will I be arrested for murder? Not an unfounded fear when bearing in mind other man's life choices. To be honest, I had no answer. It was all on file. If anyone cared to check should something like this recur, then all the information was there. He walked away from the police station without a stain on his character, but still a very worried man.

Defences

DNA has somewhat complicated matters when it comes to the field of sexual offence defences. The whole thing has changed completely due to this one single aspect.

The year is 1980. An allegation of rape is made by a young woman. Due to the sharp investigating techniques of the detectives, a name is found, and a man arrested. He is asked about the incident in an interview. All this man has to do is say, 'Not me Guv, I don't know what you are talking about. Don't know the woman, never met her.

It wasn't me, guv.' He could do this because there was nothing to link him to the woman, other than her word. Sadly, this would have applied whether he had done the deed or not.

Fast forward to 2010. The same thing happens, and a man is arrested. If the man has had sex with the woman, he can no longer say, 'wasn't me Guv'. Because if he says that and DNA is matched to him, he has nowhere to go. Instead, he would be better off at this point claiming that they had sex and that it was consensual.'

This complicates matters. In the first example, further investigation, eyewitnesses and other investigative tools would, at least, put his account into question and a case could then be built up. In the second example, you have to get inside the minds of both parties.

There are several ways we did this. One was getting a statement from the first person to see the victim after the incident. We would also get one from the first person who the victim spoke to about the attack. In the rare incidences where a woman is raped by a complete stranger, you can imagine the state of confusion and trauma she would be in afterwards. That is if she is fortunate enough to escape. She could be dishevelled and frightened. This means that the first person to come across this can give this valuable information. It is often totally independent and therefore powerful evidence. In these cases, hearsay evidence is admissible in court. Under most circumstances, one can only give evidence of what they know or have seen and heard personally. Providing evidence of what someone else said, saw or heard is hearsay evidence and for that other person to put into the evidential mix. The law-makers specifically made an exception in rape cases to enable investigators to get a flavour of her state of mind as seen by the first person to see or hear them. If the woman is – in her state of shock – shouting out things like, "He raped me, I've just been raped", taken with the general demeanour of the victim, the witness can give this evidence in court. One of the few circumstances that it is allowed. Careful analyses of injuries are helpful. Comparing the accounts to CCTV footage can be too. In fact, I once had a case where a youth attacked a much older drunk woman in her house after he offered to help her home. He told me that she could barely stand, and he had to manhandle her up two flights of stairs. CCTV of the scene showed an inebriated woman, perfectly capable of walking unaided. The youth did help her with her bags but used the lift and not the stairs. He had stated that he never went into the flat and walked away almost immediately. CCTV showed that he was upstairs for 45 minutes or more. Fingerprints had him in the hallway of the flat. DNA had him in the lounge. So, I was able to trash his account from start to finish. CPS charged the youth, but because the victim was a drunk and therefore considered unreliable, they dropped the case before it went to court. This was particularly worrying as his father had been arrested for domestic rape on several occasions, but never convicted as his wife always dropped the charges. His brother had also been investigated for similar offences. So, the young man walked away believing that he could do this sort of thing a get away with it. I fear that future dealing with him in the system are highly likely. All this means that further, thorough investigation is required in order to combine the evidential strands so that, regardless of what the forensics alone tell you, or what an interviewee says, the truth will out.

Forensics can help immensely, but cases still require a full investigation. This is where the law can work well.

I dealt with another case where a man was accused by his 40-year-old, mentally disabled niece of a rape that had purportedly happened 3 weeks earlier. The evidence was gathered, and a consistent account of a quite harrowing incident was recorded. She didn't leave her flat for two weeks immediately after the incident due to her utter confusion and not knowing what to do. A social worker had finally got hold of her and worked out what had happened. The police were called in and an investigation opened. He was arrested. He was the sort of person who thought he was more believable because he talked louder than everyone else. He was the dictionary definition of a narcissistic misogynist, and altogether a man I just didn't want to believe. It was quite difficult to maintain a professionally distanced approach. He stated, quite categorically, that he would never do that sort of thing to his own niece. The very thought turned his stomach. "She is not 'all there' She is confused. This is outrageous", he tried. "I'll have your badges for this." He was released on bail for the investigation to proceed. The officer who dealt with the victim visited her a week later when she discovered that the victim had put the sheets that had been on the bed at the time of the incident, away in the cupboard. She couldn't bring herself to touch them enough to have them washed. So, my colleague took the sheet from her and sent it off to the lab.

Yes, you guessed it. Not just his DNA was found. There was an actual semen stain on the sheet together with sperm heads (where we get the DNA) that were his exact match. As is always satisfying – what with his misogyny and all – his trial judge was a woman. He treated her the same way he treated all women, right up until he was taken down for a ten stretch.

Again, forensics worked well when combined with good detective work. Mainly from my victim liaison colleague.

When police first started collecting DNA off detainees, we had a choice of a mouth swab or 10 strands of hair with root (where the DNA is). One less-than-intelligent young man once said to me, when given this choice, that he wanted hair samples because then he was going to shave his head so we couldn't catch him again. There was not a scintilla of irony about what he said. He truly believed that his hair DNA would be different. You just can't tell some people.

Tech

Forensics doesn't just stop at fingerprints and DNA. The Met have a science lab devoted to tech. You name it, they've got it. Videos; computers; phones; the lot. The more defences demand the contents of rape victims' phones and computers, the bigger it gets. It isn't about whether or not someone did something. It is about putting doubt in the minds of jurors. What better way to do so, than to tell the world about the sexy text messages to show that the victim is clearly a hussy and not to be trusted. I will go into my views on the courts' use of this evidence in a later chapter, but I can think of only one occasion in all my years where social media messages helped prove anything, and that was to prove beyond doubt that the allegation was false.

In essence, a young lady had seduced a man to make another man, who she had the hots for, jealous. They had sex in the back of a van. And then 45 minutes later, she went to the chap who was subject of her affections, accusing the person with whom she had the liaison, of rape. He ran out to confront the villain but, as he got outside, a police car just happened past. He flagged them down and told them what he had learned. An investigation was opened. What was found in her social media messages was very revealing. A string of messages between her and her 'fall guy' about where, and when they would meet up. These went right up to the point that they actually met. There was then a 15-minute period of inactivity... at least on the social media side of things. There was then a brief exchange, mainly consisting of her telling him what a 'fine' time she had just had and that they should get together again. Less than an hour later, she stated that she hadn't actually wanted to do that and, what had actually happened was rape. In the ensuing text messages, it was almost palpable how confused and dismayed the man was. Now, I don't believe that she wanted police to be involved. She just wanted her beau to swoop in and rescue her so that they could ride off into the sunset. Once the police were involved, she couldn't back out... and never admitted to the lie. The accused man was obviously never charged, but he had been arrested before all this came out. He wasn't a good man. He actually admitted that he was a burglar, drug dealer and an altogether unpleasant person. But never rape. He would admit to murder before he would ever abuse a woman. I believed him.

Let me give you something else to consider. A colleague of mine once drafted a text that was unambiguously sexy to the point of being lurid. She then pressed send before realising that the 'Mike' that she had sent it to was not her partner, but her boss. Now, this was a toe-curling and embarrassing thing to happen. A brief and rather hurried explanation in a private conversation with the said boss settled the issue without further mention. I don't know how the story got out, but she was a 'game girl'. She came clean to all of us eventually. There was lots of chortling away in the background, but no one thought anything of it after that. What if she was then attacked on her way home that evening, or worse, her boss decided that the invitation was too tempting even though he knew it was not meant for him. Would that text then be relevant in any subsequent court case? I would say absolutely not, certainly in the case of a person other than the boss being accused. The defence would use it to destroy her credibility in either case.

I investigated a paedophile case once, where a man who had been acting inappropriately towards young boys had been caught. He tried to convince the court that the five thousand paedophilic images found on his computer had nothing to do with him. He put it to the court that it all must have been sent to his computer without his knowledge. He spent quite a while explaining all this to the court and trying to get technical in order to confuse the jury. Most important of all, he had never viewed them. Therefore, had he known they were there, he would have deleted the lot. This is where the forensic technology examiner comes in. They explained to the jury in clear, concise, and plain English exactly how the images were downloaded; how many times they had been viewed on that specific computer; how long each viewing was and just how much of a lying little toe rag he was. He had, fortunately, told us that the only other person who had access to the computer was his wife. It's not like he was going to accuse her, so he had no way to extricate himself.

The rule of thumb is that if it is on your computer, it can be found by Tech Nerds. So don't go there.

Fire Investigations

While fire investigations are normally carried out by the fire Brigades, if it involves loss of life or suspicious circumstances, the police will get involved. To this end, they have their own forensic fire investigators. These are people who appear to be able to obtain information where none exists to the untrained eye. When a crime occurs, the police like to sterilise the scene as far as possible. No one in, no one out. Nothing should be touched, moved, tampered with in any way, by anyone, for any reason until the forensic practitioners have been to photograph and examine everything. When a fire happens, you get a herd of buffaloes in the form of the Fire Brigade trampling on everything and spraying water or other fire retardants all over the precious crime scene. This can't be helped. They have to stop the fire and they have to ensure no one is trapped. The crime scene takes a back seat until the investigator comes along to find a scene of utter devastation. I followed one such investigator into a scene like this once. I was amazed at what they could divine from what they saw. I walked away from there knowing how the fire was started, where it was started, how many 'seats' of the fire there were, how long the fire lasted and many other morsels of information. All this from a scene of devastation from which any other forensic scientist would have just thrown their hands in the air and walked away.

I could bore you to tears about the individuality of tool marks at the entry points to burglaries, shoe prints, tyre marks and all manner of things. Suffice to say, the forensic examiner doesn't go to the scene of a burglary, spread a load of silvery fingerprint powder all over the place then bugger off. They have a lot more to think about and are kept busy.

Politicians

I will now go into my thoughts on politicians, as it links into much of what I have to say about other organisations. As a foreword, I want to address the fact that there will be content following this, that deals with racism. I am aware that people have differing views on this subject, and some may disagree with mine. I don't understand why the colour of one's skin would determine your character. I also don't understand why it would determine your intelligence, demeanour, nor anything else. Racism is a problem, and in order to articulate it, we must able to discuss it while catering to our different methods of expression. Therefore, I write this disclaimer in the hopes that it will be borne in mind as you continue reading.

The following will be split into two sections. The first will deal with the politicians that sit in the Houses of Parliament - 'lording it' over the hoy-polloi – and the second will deal with those sat in offices of the public service industries, such as police and NHS workers. Those who make decisions based on their own personal ambitions as opposed to those who make decisions that enhance the ability of the practitioners to do their work. It may become apparent that I don't have much faith in politicians of any variety, whatever the colour of tie they don. I don't trust them. This does not mean they are all dishonest backstabbers... I have just never come across many that aren't. It also doesn't mean that I think everyone who takes promotion is the same, just a certain type.

Politicisation of Police

When I joined, The Met was proud to proclaim that we were apolitical. The Home Office gave the police a wad of cash supplied through rates, or latterly, poll and council taxes. The Receiver – the most senior civilian employee of the Met and the one holding the purse strings – would then dish the money out to where he thought it was required. The commissioner was appointed by the Home Office but, by and large, he wasn't going any further in the job. This meant he wasn't going to be intimidated by politicians so he could make decisions based on policing needs.

Since the advent of a London Mayor and their respective responsibilities, the police are now absolutely absorbed into the political rhetoric to which each Mayor, in turn, wants to subject the service. It was a slow move over to where they are now in the political spectrum. Sir Paul Condon was probably the first commissioner in the modern era who seemed to have a political theme to his leadership. Ian Blair was the one who didn't bother to pretend otherwise. He was a Tony Blair insert, in my opinion. The position of police commissioner is now absolutely a political appointment, and they are subservient to their political masters.

Now, all of this may seem trivial. Perhaps the police should just get on with it and never mind the politics. The problem is, whenever the media get hot under the collar about something, politicians start worrying about their personal profile. They then start messing around with statistics. They then put pressure on the police to target whatever is going to enhance their ambitions. This, in turn, affects where senior officers deploy their troops.

Stop and search policy

Take, for example, stop and search. A subject that's full of opinion, emotion and political rhetoric. It has been said for the last 35 years, that I know of, that the police abuse their powers of stop and search and a disproportionate number of people from the ethnic minority community are targeted. Where do we go with that? Essentially, what happened initially was that police were actively discouraged from performing any stop and search at all. The catchphrase was always 'intelligence-led policing'. There is a small problem with that, but before I go into that, the result was that very few people got searched. Many known criminals were effectively allowed to wander around armed to the teeth in the knowledge that the police wouldn't search them.

Now we fast forward to 2016 and beyond where knife crime is prevalent in the media. Many reports describe it as an epidemic. The media seemed happy that the rest of the world felt that the entire of England were drowning in a pool of blood caused by about 20 youths a year falling victim. The President of the USA – a country whose figures for fatal violent incidents in most *cities* outstrip the number of fatalities caused by criminal actions in the entire of the UK – has decided that London is too dangerous for Americans. This probably has more to do with the fact that the Mayor is Islamic, a group of people some believe is despised by the current President… .but hey, that's the media for you.

So, now politicians are in a quandary. They don't want police to stop and search of ethnic minorities and they don't want youths dying in the streets of London. We can all remember the trouble the Police Commissioner Paul Condon had when he, probably as a result of a Home Office directive, stated that most robberies were committed by young black males. An accurate statement whether we like it or not. But he was, of course, accused of racism. The political point scorers twisted his words so that they sounded as if he was saying that most black youths were robbers. He never said that, never meant that, never intended that anyone should think that. What he meant to say (from my point of view) is that the statistics were giving us a starting point. What he was saying, was that this was where we, as a society, should tackle why this demographic have been put into this position by our lack of understanding that has led them into such a lifestyle. What is society doing that has caused them to become so marginalised that they resort to these acts? Politicians are never going to help in this. They are not concerned with societal causes. They are only interested in the look, and more specifically, their look.

Here is the problem with intelligence-led policing. The intelligence will tell us that the overwhelming majority of people dying through knife crime are young black males. The overwhelming majority of people wielding the knives that kill these victims are young black males. This isn't my opinion, it's fact. It's in bold print everywhere you look. Every statistic in the country will confirm this. This is not to say that most members of ethnic minority groups are knife-wielding maniacs, that is demonstrably untrue. However, if someone approaches the police and says, "I've just been stabbed, he went off in that direction. He was a young skinny black guy", would we then expect the police to go around stopping and searching 50-year-old fat white guys looking for Rodney Robber as we shall call him? I think not. Like it or not, intelligence-led policing will lead the police to stop and search a 'disproportionate' number of black youths. It is only disproportionate in terms of the number of black youths when compared with the number of people in the country. Not when compared to the number of people falling victim to, and causing these issues. We also have to consider that many complaints about this disproportionate number of stop and searches occur in areas populated by ethnic minorities, which adds another factor in the mix of ascertaining what is, or is not, disproportionate.

So there we have it. Politicians want quick fixes and, as a result, police have to carry out those quick fixes. Which aren't actually quick fixes at all because there is no such thing. The way to deal with this particular problem is re-education of those whose belief is that these youngsters must be in a gang. Make no mistake, the overwhelming majority of both victims and offenders in this area are gang members or at the very least wannabe gang members.

Police are employed to prevent and detect crime and to keep the queen's peace. They are not there to divert youngsters that are going off the rails. This is a job for Social Services, in combination with parents and teachers, assisted by information supplied by the police. So, when people on TV to complain about police stop and search powers, telling the world that there are better ways to deal with the issue, well... yes there is. Police have a job to do. Being social workers is not one of them. Having meetings with social workers is. Persuading the social services to act upon these issues is another level entirely

The Politicisation of Robbery

One of the offences that got all politicians hopping was robbery. Robbery is specifically theft with violence, or the threat thereof. When I went to school, I was given a lunch box with sandwiches and some small change for the tuck shop. In the 80s and 90s, kids were probably going to school with something similar. If someone was subject to the attentions of the local school bully, he would have his 50p taken from him. His sandwiches would end up with a big old boot print in them. The victim would then go running home and tearfully tell his Mother. She would brush him down and Dad would work out ways of getting his son to fight back. It would then be forgotten ... until the next time. This sort of thing is technically a robbery, but it would never be reported. Too much like hard work for a few pennies and a sandwich. In the modern era, the kids are walking around with hundreds of pounds plus worth of tech and often more cash than they would ever need. This means that when it is taken off them by the local school bully, it seldom goes under the radar. The parents can't simply ignore it. It has to be reported for insurance purposes. So, police get called, they investigate and a robbery allegation is recorded.

Where it was never being reported but was probably happening as much as it is now, the stats show that robbery has spiked hugely. If that is the case, something has to be done. We can't have politicians being shown as wanting. So now what we have is an entire unit staffed by uniformed officers, detectives, Sergeants, Inspectors and civilian staff – all to deal with 15-year-old Rodney Robber who is going around nicking mobile phones off 13-year-old boys – who probably nicked them off a 12-year-old earlier that day. The parents seem to think their kids have to have the tech in case they get into trouble. They don't understand that it is the tech that is getting them into trouble in the first place. So, when Mummy says, "my little Tarquin needs an £800 phone. I would hate it if he was in trouble and had no way of contacting me!" I have to respond by saying, "if little Tarquin found himself in trouble, it would be because of his phone and he wouldn't be able to contact you because someone else will have it!" Believe it or not, there is no telling these people. Let's face it, these kids have probably persuaded their parents to get the latest tech because they don't want to be seen with a naff phone.

The Flying Squad (Sweeney) was set up to deal with armed robberies in the 70s. Can you imagine John Thaw and Co in the 1970's TV series of the same name (apologies to the youngsters if this is before your time, you will have to watch *The Sweeney* on 'catch-up' to get the reference), crashing into some 15-year-old oik's bedroom and saying, "get yer trousers on, you're nicked!" for a mobile phone.

Statistics and League Tables

In my own forewarning fashion, this subject that really gets my goat. During the reign of Tony Blair, the idea of gathering statistics to create league tables and essentially put everyone into competition with each other was born. I don't blame Blair for coming up with the concept – although I am always happy to point accusatory fingers at him any other time. It had more to do with computerisation. In the 80s and 90s, if you wanted to know what was happening in a particular area of public life, you had to go into the archives. This would be an actual room, not a website. You would then have to collect reams of papers and go through them by hand. You collected whatever figures you needed by reading through each paper. You would then need to extrapolate these numbers, compare and contrast and come up with some sort of result. It was time-consuming, labour intensive and, perhaps most concerning of all, inaccurate. There were entire departments dedicated to this sort of stuff. Then computers became an intrinsic part of our lives. Stats could be obtained at the press of a button, and the computer would do all the work for you. Easy and accurate.

The problem was that everything was about the stats. Those numbers were pretty meaningless most of the time. I am aware that in the teaching profession, stats are used to describe schools in terms of their successes or failures. There are too many examples of 'successful' schools that really should never be allowed to continue in the way that they do. There are also many other 'failing' schools that are doing a perfectly good job. The difference between the two is that the headteacher of the 'successful' school will spend all their time manipulating the stats in their favour, and the head of the 'failing' school will spend all their time educating the students, thereby neglecting the stats.

The police do not escape this phenomenon, this is an issue that most people know nothing about even though it affects their daily lives. So this is the issue. The criminal Investigation side of police work is judged on 'clear-ups', meaning that any allegation made is investigated. If it results in someone being charged or cautioned, it is deemed as a success. Any other result is considered a failed investigation. In the meantime, the CPS are judged on convictions at court. They are also the arbiters of what actually goes to court. The police v have to get the authority to charge from this body in all serious cases. All very well, but it does mean that if the CPS are a bit concerned that a case won't succeed at court, they will act as the judge and jury and drop the case. They have become an unelected organisation who makes decisions that the law of this country states should be taken by a jury. And the reason is stats and, more specifically, ones that suggest 'success'.

If we look at clear ups, they will show an equally inaccurate picture. There are many reasons why an investigation does not go to court. Some are to do with inadequate police investigations, but this is a relatively small part of it. I could go off and investigate an incident and come back to my boss being able to give him chapter and verse of the incident. What happened, when it happened, how it happened, what the suspect's second-cousin-twice-removed had for breakfast three weeks prior. If the victim doesn't want to go to court, the suspect won't be charged, and it will be shown as a 'failed' investigation. If my investigation shows that there were no offences committed – like the little old lady who thinks her carer has nicked her purse, then finds it intact a week later stuffed down the side of the chair that she sits in – it will still be shown as a failed investigation. I could have everything... evidence pointing to the suspect, victim's statements and willingness, witnesses, CCTV, the lot. Nevertheless, the CPS decide they don't want to charge, it is shown as a 'failed' investigation. Strangely, if it does go through the system and the suspect is acquitted at court, it is still shown as a 'success' for me as the person had been charged. Perhaps now we begin to see the inherent flaws in our legal system.

These stats not only do not tell the whole story, they actually give an inaccurate picture. Problem is that politicians rely on it.

All of this filters down to police officers and their supervisors. Inspectors – at least those who are a relatively short way into their careers – will always have one eye on their next promotion. It is for this reason they become the office-type politicians. I walked into my Inspector's office late one evening when he had gone home. I noticed that he had a league table of the officers on his wall. I was on the top so, in his world, the most successful. I tore the whole thing down and binned it. It never went back up. My issue was, that we all worked as a team and successes should be seen as a team effort. This way, the office has unity and is a happier existence. This is, of course, as opposed to everyone being in competition with each other. No one helps their colleagues, no one feels the successes, and the efficiency of the office takes a tumble. That is without taking into account the working environment. Yes, I had a lot of successes, and they outnumbered the failures. I did, however, feel that those failures were sometimes the result of our failure to work as a team. I would always take them and learn from them, but I often felt the successes were so was because of the joint effort.

This sort of thing cannot be measured on a computer. If I had a 'clear up', it was my success. The other people working on that investigation were ignored. The numbers would show that they were 'failing' when they absolutely were not. Now, I do know that if you look at the figures over a long period of time, then pictures for individuals can become apparent, but the politicians don't care about that, they want immediacy. An Inspector will only be in position for a year or two before they are moved onward and upward, so a rolling statistic that continues for longer than that will be of no use to what is of importance in their lives. Somewhat unfortunately, but understandably, their next promotion.

When talking of the senior police officers. The ones responsible for decisions made in all areas of police work, we have to understand that they are not experts in the field of criminal investigation. We have all seen police dramas on TV. The heroes tend to be Inspectors (Frost), Chief Inspectors (Morse), Superintendents (Was that a Helen Mirren role?) all the way up to Chief Constable. In the real world, nothing is further from the truth. In the 90s, Inspectors and Chief Inspectors had their conditions of service changed. It was all put to the vote across the entire country. Did these ranks want to remain on an hourly rate (which meant they could earn overtime), or become salaried? They were given a carrot. All affected ranks would be earning an extra £3000 a year as compensation for the loss of overtime. All those Inspectors who were pushing paperclips around an office on the 12th floor of New Scotland Yard (NSY) and couldn't remember when they last earned over time, or the country bumpkins who couldn't remember the last time investigated anything, jumped at the chance. They weren't earning overtime, so it was £3000 that they didn't have before. To the relatively small minority of working DIs and DCIs in London, Manchester, the West Midlands and other large cities, this represented a rather devastating pay cut. Many worked all hours and were earning 3 times that in overtime every year. Of course, the majority won the day. What this meant was that all those working DIs suddenly stopped working overtime. They stopped going out on raids with the troops. They stopped doing anything hands-on. Many of the duties considered the preserve of the Senior Investigating Officer (SIO), devolved downward. Even legislation was changed so that where the law insisted that Inspectors had to do things, it would become a little bit more of a grey area until it became common-practise that DCs would now do the job under supervision.

The upshot was that DIs and DCIs did not investigate anything. Detective Constables became the lead. The Sergeants supervised and, when they weren't knee-deep in computer-based supervision, they would sneak out on some enquiries. But never DIs. The DCI didn't leave the office unless it' was to go home. They even conferenced over the phone. All these TV Inspectors going out arresting people and interviewing them and taking statements and the like? Never happens. I know of two occasions where Inspectors made an arrest in the last 30 years and one was just going out to grab some lunch and fell upon an incident. Wrong place wrong time. Of course, he got someone else to book the detainee in and that was it. A quick statement and hand it down.

So, all they do now is supervise and rubber-stamp decisions made by Detective Constables (DC) and Detective Sergeants (DS), dreaming of ways to boost his or her chances of climbing the greasy promotion pole. They will claim responsibility for all the 'successful' outcomes and distance themselves from the 'failures'. Just like a politician. Obviously, there were some, normally approaching the end of their careers and not intending on going any higher that tended to make better decisions. They were advantaged by the fact that they had been there, done it and got the t-shirt. They also weren't worried about what the senior officers thought. As long as they didn't completely cock it all up, it was fine.

One of the more annoying results of this, combined with the results base scrutiny we were all put under, was that once a case had been authorised by the CPS for a charge, senior police officers had their little tick in the box. They then had no more interest in the case. As far as the investigating officers were concerned, they were only halfway through the investigation. It only stopped when the case had gone to court. As far as senior officers were concerned, it was a CPS issue now. All the work that had to be done after the person was charged was never considered when deciding how effective a particular officer was. Of course, if the CPS needed extra work doing on the case or a new piece of information had come to hand or the defence wanted something, it was not they that did the leg work. Oh, no. That was down to the investigator. So, our esteemed supervisors were only interested in half of the job that we did. If the case was successful at court, the CPS would lord it up and tell everyone what a wonderful job they had done. Our supervisors would think nothing either way. If it was not a success, the CPS would claim that the officer's investigation was lacking and even go as far as to try to have the person disciplined in serious cases. Our supervisors would just comply but have no real interest. After all, they had their little box nicely ticked.

Crown Prosecution Service (CPS)

This is the organisation responsible for getting all criminal cases through the courts. They are the prosecuting lawyers. As such, they make all the decisions about who does and doesn't get their say in court. So, when I felt I had sufficient evidence to charge with a rape case, I had to put the paperwork together for them to make a decision.

So far, so good. It must be said that they were there to authorise charges, state what they were, then take on the case and get it through the court. They weren't there to make any other decisions in terms of the first part of the investigation. Once the decision was made to charge, my job changed from being an independent investigator to a prosecuting agent. Any further work required was done by me. For example, if new evidence came to light casting doubt on a case, I would switch back to being an investigator. I would then deal with whatever needed to be dealt with. I would then pass it back to the CPS for a decision. Whether or not to continue always remained ultimately, and firmly in fact, in their hands.

Unfortunately, many DIs did not understand this. It was their job to supervise and drive the investigation forward. If I felt that there would never be sufficient evidence to charge, I would not go to the CPS because their job was to authorise charges only. If I didn't think there was sufficient evidence, why on earth would I bother them? Nevertheless, some DI's simply would not. Whether they were too afraid to make decisions, I don't know... but something tells me it has to do with the risk that their little tick boxes might remain empty. So I would go to the DI and tell them everything about the case and get them to make a decision to take no further action. I can't tell you how many times I had to then go to the CPS for a 'charging decision' knowing that they were never going to do that. The CPS thought that I was chancing my arm trying to get a dodgy decision past them, when I was agreeing with them I actuality. In the sexual offences department of the CPS, they were inundated with cases. Each individual lawyer had over a hundred cases to deal with at any one time, so they didn't need that extra workload. It could be said that much of the workload could have been reduced by being a little more efficient and not dragging their feet with every decision going... but it wouldn't take away the fact that there was too much work and not enough lawyers.

The upshot was that the CPS got fed up. They started insisting that the paperwork for them to make a decision had to be completed to a point where the whole case could, in theory, go to court with no further work. Though this appears sensible, it often meant a great deal of time and administrative work was spent on cases that might not even end up going to court. It was therefore needless because the CPS would often end up saying that there was not enough evidence. Hours of time and resources spent when they could be used elsewhere. They were there to decide if there was enough evidence but wouldn't do it if all the admin stuff that had no bearing on the evidence wasn't done. Very frustrating, and all because those who were there to make decisions, wouldn't. And the reason why they wouldn't was because of meaningless statistics that they felt would ruin their chances of their next promotion. Something that I couldn't care less about.

It wasn't just police that were chasing their tails running after these stats. The CPS were just as much a part of the system, so also fell victim to decision-making pressure based on short-sighted political rhetoric.

Domestics

A subject from which everyone wants to shy away. No one wants to interfere when warring parties are at each other's throats, metaphorically or physically... but we have to. Like sexual offences, the police didn't cover themselves in glory in the past, so decisions had to be taken out of their hands. It was decided that in all domestic assault cases, there should be a 'positive action' policy to ensure that something, anything, would be done. Some Inspectors thought this meant that in all cases, an arrest had to be made if the suspect was there. A 'positive arrest' policy. This may sound alright, but it isn't. A senior ranking officer could not come up to me and say, "You! Arrest that man over there!". At least not without giving me all the information and satisfying me that there were sufficient grounds for that arrest. If I was making the arrest, it was for me to justify it, not some jumped up DI who couldn't be asked to do it himself. This meant that I needed to know everything. It happened to me once. A DI and a DS tried to gang up on me to arrest a man when I knew there was not enough evidence. I knew this because I had investigated it, and the evidence showed that the person was definitely not guilty of anything. I refused. The DI tried to discipline me and failed because I was correct in my actions. So, if an individual officer can't do that, you certainly could not have an over-arching, blanket policy suggesting that all suspects should be arrested. Each incident needed to be investigated on its own merits.

I had to deal with a domestic where a guy had come home to find his girlfriend had turned into a whirling dervish in his absence. Something had wound her up. Not wishing to hang around, he decided that he would beat a retreat and went to grab some essentials from the bedroom. She followed him up and physically attacked him to prevent him from packing his stuff. "Well," he thought, "sod this for a game of soldiers, I'll go without my stuff". He then started to make his way to the front door. She blocked his way and refused to let him go. She attacked him every time he tried. So he eventually just grabbed her by the waist, picked her up, and put her to one side so he could get to the door. He was then able to make his retreat away from the violence. She then called the police and made an allegation of assault. The reporting officer stated that there was a slight reddening to her cheek, which she put down to his assault. I personally couldn't see it at all when I spoke to her. Apparently, it could be seen in good sunlight at a certain angle if you looked hard enough. Anyway, a massive manhunt was launched into this crazed, maniacal attacker and he was found about 15 minutes later at a friend's house. Police went in and arrested him. When I saw him, I could see that he had deep scratches around his neck, a gouge out of his face, bruises from defence wounds on his arms, and torn clothes. He was a mess, and it was caused by her. Of course, he wouldn't press charges, it isn't the sort of thing 'geezers' do. But why arrest him when he was not the aggressor and was, in fact, the injured party. He had even taken his own 'positive action' by removing himself from the address. So, because the young officers were effectively being bullied into making an arrest, they ended up arresting a victim instead of a suspect. So no, I didn't agree with this way of dealing with the issues. There are many other ways to get a positive result without doing this.

The CPS had similar issues. They had a 'positive charging' policy. If it was domestic, it would be a charge for some of the lawyers, regardless of evidential considerations.

Domestic rape. Something that should always be dealt with properly and effectively. It must be a horrible place in which to find yourself when your home, the place that you should consider your safe place, is the one place that you feel in the most danger. This case involved a lady of foreign extraction. She could speak no English, so everything was done through an interpreter. Whether it was cultural issues, embarrassment or something entirely different, we could not get her to tell us anything other than, "he raped me." When asked if this was just the one time or more, she said, "many times." That was the extent of the information we could get. Some of the most skilful and experienced interviewers could not get through. I didn't know where it happened, when it happened, how it happened, what went in where (it makes a difference, believe me) or who was there. I knew nothing, "he raped me", "many times."

He denied everything and stated that she had just married him to get into the country. Once this was achieved, she didn't want anything more to do with him. I don't know if this was true or not. It didn't make any difference, if I couldn't get any details out of her, I couldn't investigate, and I could never get to the facts. I didn't have any. Forensics couldn't help. They were man and wife so his DNA would be all over the place. There were no witnesses, she knew no one and had told no one anything. We believed that it all took place at home, so no CCTV evidence.

. nothing. After weeks of trying different interviewers, interview sites and just trying anything to get something to hang my hat on, I gave up and went to the DI to get a decision as to how long this could go on before we had to abandon it. It would never be completely abandoned, but we had to say to her, give us the information in your own time and we will take it forward. Until then, we can do nothing. The DI was too frightened to make that decision, so I had to spend days putting together a case that the CPS could make a decision on, knowing that there was nothing for them to consider. To my astonishment, the CPS rep said that they had a 'positive charging policy' and she could not do anything other than charge the man.

All this meant that I went to court for a rape case where I had no evidence what so ever. Everyone was looking at me asking what on earth I was doing bringing this case to court. The CPS were conspicuous by their absence and left everything to the poor barrister. Naturally, the jury had no problem in acquitting the defendant. He didn't have to say anything because there was no allegation to put to him. This was a lot of time and effort for no return whatsoever. All because of political decision making that made no sense.

I had a reasonably good working relationship with the CPS reps in my part of town. They knew that I got them the results that made them look good, so they were prepared to give a little back. I think part of the problem that police and CPS had was their mutual inefficiency. CPS would demand all the paperwork on their desks five minutes before they make the demand. Many police were just not good at keeping up with the paperwork, and the CPS were chaotic because of the ridiculously high workload resulting in said paperwork often being lost. It isn't like they left it all on a train or anything. They never took the stuff out of the office. It was just that it was too much like hard work to look for it in the bombsite that was the CPS offices. It was much easier to accuse the police of not handing the papers to them in the first place and get them to do it again. I always kept a full copy of everything I handed over and an electronic record of every time I communicated with them. That meant they couldn't do that to me. Didn't stop some of them from trying though. It was always quite amusing when a DI came into the office wagging accusative fingers at me about my lack of efficiency only to find me waving evidence to the contrary back at him.

Another decision that I thought a little weird was one involving drugs. A bunch of 18-year-old kids were stopped on their way back home to Brighton from the centre of London. The car was searched and 198 ecstasy pills were found in a single box. They were arrested and admitted to the possession. They stated that they got them from someone just outside Brighton and went to London to check out the club scene and have a good time. They were on their way back when they were stopped and they had, as near as makes no difference, no money on them. They were sober, helpful and very concerned for their futures. They were actually arrested for possession with intent to supply based on the amount that they had on them.

I took it to the CPS for a decision on possession only. Everyone thought I was mad but, here's the thing. They bought a box of 200 pills and had clearly used two. And they were going back home. This would suggest that if they were indeed supplying, they would have had a lot fewer tablets and a shed load more money. Either they were the worst salespeople in the world, or they weren't supplying. No one can tell me they wouldn't have found dozens of willing buyers in and around Soho and Leicester Square. So, I came to the conclusion that they cannot have been out there selling their wares. They must have been in possession of them for some other reason. Maybe they didn't want to leave them at home in case Mum or Dad, or worse, Brother found them. I don't know... but they weren't supplying. The CPS took a different point of view and charged them with possession with intent. They elected to go for trial by jury and 6 months later we were all gathered at the Crown Court to await the start of proceedings. Then the prosecuting barrister pulled me to one side and whispered in my ear, "Do you really think this is a possession with intent?" I, of course, said what I had been saying all along. "No, we haven't a snowball's chance in hell of convicting these guys." "I agree," said the barrister. He then toddled off to speak to the CPS, who still had the final decision in these cases and succeeded where I failed in persuading them of the correct course.

The case was opened, and the charges amended to reflect common sense. The drug barons pleaded guilty, thanked me for my handling of the case and then walked off into the sunset reformed characters one and all.

Casting back to another issue we've come across in this piece. Sexual offences against sex workers happen. I only know of one time when someone was charged and convicted of this type of offence in a brothel, and I am proud to proclaim that it was I who investigated the whole thing. It is also the only time I have ever been in a knocking shop. Briefly, the premises were accessed by a stairway that was immediately in front of you as you entered the front door. Halfway up the stairs is a locked metal gate so that the ladies could control who came and went. A strict one-at-a-time policy was enforced. There were CCTV cameras at the gate and on the first floor. The business took place on the second floor, where modesty forbade the use of cameras.

A man entered the building and was allowed through. He spent about 5 minutes on the second floor speaking to a woman, obviously flexing his negotiating skills. He then left. 15 minutes later, he returned. As he was halfway through the gate, he stopped, preventing them from closing it. A friend then came in through the front door as part of a clear plan to get both of them in there at the same time. They then both forced their way in brushing aside the protestations of the madam. There then followed a very threatening passage of time. They intimidated the ladies to give up the location of their cash stash. The one who seemed to take the lead ripped the entry camera off the wall, not realising that there were other cameras dotted around all wired for sound. They had a security man who was as useful as a chocolate teapot. One of the intruders had grabbed a snooker cue off the security man and used this to intimidate the ladies. He then demanded money, which they told him they didn't have. The intruder then said that he would take it in kind and sexually assaulted the madam, being decent enough to do this on camera for all to see both his actions and her refusal to consent. He then made them go upstairs. The girls raised their voices while they were out of camera shot ostensibly to show nervousness but actually to ensure the CCTV was picking up what was going on upstairs. By now, police had been called by one of the women who had been out and just returned to find she couldn't get in. She could hear what was happening. At the same time as the police tried to gain entry through the gate, the madam was being raped. This was out of shot of the cameras, but everything could be heard. It was all quite distressing. The police eventually got in. One of the men made good his escape through a window but was caught later, the other was arrested on the scene.

The interview was interesting because I didn't tell him that the cameras were wired for sound. When I eventually did, halfway through the interview, he got the right hump and immediately fired his solicitor. He then tried to front it out on his own. Didn't work. He was screwed in so many different ways. At least I didn't have to put up with the smirk on his face that he maintained prior to my revelation.

The reason why I put this under this heading is because of the CPS thought process. Obviously, we had a load of very nervous women who treated authority with suspicion, so we had to treat these ladies with kid gloves. What we were dealing with was a pair of robbers who, having not discovered the stash, went with rape instead. We remember that rape is not about sex, it is about power, control and the removal of choice. Well, this is what robbery is about as well. Burglars burgle because they need cash, robbers rob because they need to have power over others. What they steal is often by the by. Not a surprising leap to go from robbery to rape if you have that sort of attitude.

When I had my consultation with the CPS rep, she could obviously not deny that there were clear offences that were proven. So, she did authorise rape charges. But then she asked me what I was doing about the brothel. What she wanted was for me to gather information to look at whatever offences the women were committing. I told her in language that brooked no argument, that if that was to happen, I would have nothing to do with it. It would have been a conflict of interest. I don't use prostitutes and I know all about the illegal aspects. However, this house was clean, well run and afforded a safe place for people who would otherwise be on the street and had a strict no drugs policy. Yes, they were nudging a few laws around, but they weren't harming anyone. And it was not as serious as robbery and rape.

I did have a conversation with the madam and told her of the conversation and that I would personally not investigate anything surrounding the running of this house of ill-repute. I didn't need to tell her about the law, she wasn't stupid. I told her that nothing would happen until the case was completed but that I would not be able to stop any investigation after that. Nor could I lie if I was asked about it in an official capacity. I wouldn't volunteer the information, but I wouldn't withhold it either. The CPS came around to my way of thinking. The ladies gave evidence in court. I know sex workers are not ones to respect some of our laws and are not always honest. But when it comes to the physical workings of sexual acts, they are brutally honest. So the evidence was clear, concise and consistent. You would have to wake up early in the morning to embarrass these ladies. The CCTV nailed it for us and, despite two dissenters in the jury who obviously couldn't care less about something as serious as rape and saw prostitution as a much more serious offence, he was convicted on a majority decision.

I don't know what happened to the ladies after the case. I imagine, they quietly slipped out of the premises that they used and found another one nearby. Good luck to them. They provide a service, make a living, and assisted us in our work more than many of our other victims. They harm no one..

Courts

This is where it can get controversial. The majority of my Crown Court cases were rapes and serious sexual assaults. Historically, these cases do not enjoy a high success rate when it comes to jury decisions. When I investigated these offences, I always tried to make sure that I was present when decisions were made. Whether it was the DI, the CPS, or decisions made by judges. I was always available to stand up for the victim. Here, we have to bear in mind that once a case is charged and on its way to court, I have no trouble in believing the victim. I have done my investigation. The facts have pointed me in that direction. I become a part of the prosecution team unless, or until, any new evidence pops up that casts doubt. In these cases, I just revert back to the investigator – believe no one, question everything – and find the truth. I can recall at least one occasion when the CPS decided to drop a case before it got to court and tried to exclude me from the decision. I was, in fact, tipped off by a court clerk who was surprised that I was not at court. In order to have a case dropped, the CPS have to put their case to the judge, who would have presided over the proceedings. If they were not willing to carry on with the case, the last thing they need was me sticking my oar in and putting a counter-argument. They usually got their way, but if it had got that far, I normally had a belief and did not want to see someone get away with it.

Rape Cases

It is my view, one I believe is shared widely throughout the legal sphere, that the courts deal with rape cases very badly. This is even to the point where, I believe, justice is often not done. As investigators, we understand that the subject matter is difficult, embarrassing and emotionally draining for genuine victims of these offences. We go to great lengths to try to make people as comfortable as we can. We may as well ask them to sleep on a bed of nails, but we try.

All of our efforts are basically trashed as soon as the court opens. It seems that rape victims are fair game. The defence are allowed to cast aspersions on their character – not whether they are honest or not, they don't care about that – they are interested in their sexual appetite. This, they say, goes to the heart of the matter. If the woman enjoys sex, then it must mean that anyone can have a go. That is what it seems to me, and it is wrong. Rape is when a man has sex with someone without their explicit and willing consent. That is all there is to it. It matters not if the person wanted sex with him the day before, or even earlier the same day. Nor does it matter if the person wanted sex with Manchester United. If they don't want it now, then you don't get to overrule their decision. Sex workers can and do get raped on a regular basis. This happens because the men know that juries would take a dim view of their history and essentially tell them that it is their fault for doing what they do. Yes, they can put themselves in danger, but if they say no, then no it is. A bloke cannot say, "well, you agreed yesterday, that is good enough for me today."

Unfortunately, the defence will want to know who the woman has had sexual congress with, what messages they have sent to the defendant or anyone else. They will claim that a saucy text message is tantamount to an acceptance. It should not work like that. If I was in the habit of giving mobile phones away to complete strangers and some random bloke comes up and helps himself after I have told him not to, that is my decision, and no one would think of denying that. Because I say he can have a phone today, it doesn't mean he can stroll up every other day and take what he wants. This seems obvious, so why would it not be the same for women – or men for that matter. Although I have seen little evidence of male rape victims undergoing the kind of treatment that courts dish out to women. This may, of course, be because these cases aren't as common.

In any event, I think they need to drag themselves into the 21st century.

Now for the bad news. In any trial, the jury – those '12 good men and true,' the ones that make the final decision on all Crown Court cases – are the people with the least knowledge of the case. The trial judge is appointed quite early in the proceedings. They will have access to all paperwork from the prosecution and the defence. The police will have a defence case statement detailing what they're going to try to convince the jury. They will then investigate the defence's claims and learn what they can. The defence team will have access to all documents appropriate to their defence and some more besides. Even the people in the gallery will have a view of the entire proceedings. The jury, however, are sent out whenever there is a point of law to discuss. The defence will often have pieces of evidence disallowed so that the jury never gets to hear the full case. It is not unusual for juries to have only 50% of the available evidence. I personally don't think that is right. If it is evidence, then surely the jury should decide. They are the ones that should make a decision on whether an item is prejudicial to the defence! Prejudicial! How is that possible? The word literally means 'before justice' and means that someone is making a decision before they've heard all the evidence. If you are standing in the courtroom, halfway through a trial, how can it be prejudice? If the jury has to make their decision before being allowed to hear evidence because the judge has disallowed it, I would say that is closer to the meaning of prejudice than not allowing them to take actual evidential events into account. Anyway, surely that is what prosecution evidence is – damning to the defence. That is what it is for, isn't it?

A man is attacked in the street by a knife-wielding maniac. At least that is what I was once presented with as an allegation. The attacker tried to stab the man in the eye. He missed and got him on the eyebrow, causing a deep laceration. When I say victim, I have to qualify that. He was a prominent and well-connected member of the darker side of our society and an unpleasant character, who had probably ruined many lives in his long and illustrious career. As it happened, a local resident was awakened by the disturbance and saw the incident and saw the attacker make his getaway in a red BMW. He recorded the registration number of the car and contacted police. I took a statement from the man, but could not take the item on which he had recorded the number. I told him that he needed to keep it safe and make it available for investigative purposes and for evidential purposes during the trial. The description of the suspect was distinctive. I found a name, address and telephone number for the suspect and contacted him. I asked him to come to the police station so that the investigation could be taken to the next level. The description was so distinctive, that I spotted him in a very busy front office standing at the back of a large group of people. I was confident that this was the attacker. He was eventually charged, and the case went to the Crown Court. In the meantime, our witness had a touch of the seconds. He didn't want to go to court anymore. He was told in no uncertain terms that if the court wanted him there, he had no choice. He attended court on the allotted day but had conveniently lost the item he was supposed to keep safe. The one with the registration number of the car.

"No problem," says the prosecutor. "He called the police to report this and that call was recorded. The recording should be available and the registration number should be in there somewhere." So, on the day of trial, I had to get to NSY to pick up the recording. I returned with said recording and we found a private room in which to play the tape. Whenever someone dials 999, the conversation is not just recorded, the operator will type out everything that was said. This means that there will be a computer record which should reflect the telephone conversation. When we listened to the tape, we found it was entirely blank. Whatever had happened, it hadn't recorded. So we had to go into the court with no physical proof of the registration number of the car. The jury heard the evidence without this vital piece of information. At least, until it came to the interview with the suspect. In most circumstances, a transcript of the recorded interview of all suspects is read out at court. It is seen by all parties beforehand, and if anyone objects to anything, the judge can make a decision and have the offending passages redacted if necessary. In this case, the entire interview was agreed – including the bit where I read out the registration number of the car. So, I now have this information in evidence. Phew! One of the more astute jurors then sent a note to the judge asking where the number came from. It hadn't been heard of before. No evidence was given as to how it was obtained. So quite rightly, he was confused. The jury was asked to leave the court while this was discussed. When they returned the judge told them that they simply had to 'un-remember' (this is in quotation marks for a reason, I am actually quoting the judge here) that piece of evidence. Make-believe it had never happened.

The trial came to an end and, as is the practice, the prosecutor summed up his evidence followed by the defence. The judge then had his two penn'orth before the jury was sent out to consider their verdict. In the defence's summing-up, the barrister stated that the police had been told that the attacker was a black man driving a red BMW. Armed only with this information, the police went out and stopped the first red BMW being driven by a black person and built a case up around him. Now, this was a bare-faced lie being told in front of me, the prosecutor and the judge, all of whom would have known it was a lie. Yet nothing was said to correct this. It seems witnesses are not allowed to lie as they will be sent to prison. The defendant and his representative, however, are at liberty to say whatever they please knowing that they won't be challenged. The jury then went into their discussions not only not having all the evidence but also having an outright lie ringing in their ears.

Here is the thing. The defendant was hitherto a decent upstanding member of the community, who worked hard and had no previous police issues of any description. He was actually a very likeable chap. The victim was everything he wasn't. I never found out what turned a perfectly decent man into a 'knife-wielding maniac', but I can use my imagination and I reckon this 'victim' has led a niece of this man astray and ruined her life. This was revenge. He got away with it as the jury acquitted him. I wasn't entirely unhappy with the result. Sometimes justice comes from a slightly different angle.

The Jury

Despite what the powers-that-be would like us to think, trial by jury is a popularity contest. There are some jurors that try their best to assess the evidence and come to decisions based on that alone. They are, however, fighting an uphill battle. Most jurors go into their deliberations at the end of a trial with a clear idea of their verdict. This will often be based on how the people giving evidence – be they victims, witnesses or defendants – came across, and not necessarily what they said. I have watched many jury panels and have been on two. I could tell when they were interested in the evidence of witnesses. The more attention they gave, the more weight they were going to give that evidence. The only thing that I found entirely consistent with all of them was, as they came into the court to deliver the verdict, if more than two looked directly at the defendant, it was going to be a 'not guilty' verdict. If none looked at the defendant, it was a 'guilty' one.

Let's keep it controversial and talk about professional juries. I can see even now, civil rights activists, lawyers, and all manner of people going into meltdown at the very mention of this but, bear with me, I will explain.

It is my view that professional jurors should be employed in two specific types of cases. "What cases would these be?" I hear you ask. Could it be murder-most-foul, the most serious of offences that juries get to decide on? No. Murder is a straightforward concept that even the most simple-minded of people can grasp. A person walking around whistling a happy tune one moment, dead in a ditch the next with a dozen stab wounds to his heart. That is murder. All you have to prove is that the attacker meant to cause 'serious' injury and, as a result of that injury, the victim dies. It is even easier than trying to prove attempted murder. For this, you have to prove an intent to take life and a physical act that would have, if fully completed, achieved that aim. However, it is still an easy concept that all people understand.

So not murder. Complex fraud, however, is something that some of the most intelligent people get bamboozled by. Fraudsters are, by nature, charmers. They are believable and they make sure that the trail they leave is as complicated as possible so that the victim often doesn't even know what has happened. I have investigated some of the less complicated frauds and found it all to be smoke and mirrors. Difficult to grasp. Like trying to catch the wind to paraphrase Mr Neil Young.

These trials can go on for months and more. The jurors, most of whom are Mr and Mrs average, are often lost at day one. They are expected to take in everything that experts find difficult to understand, making some kind of sensible decision at the end of it. It isn't fair on the jurors, and it isn't fair on the public who have to accept these people back into society after they are acquitted. Oh and please don't believe that the justice system will make allowances for people who will never understand this. Quite the reverse, the more they can confuse and bewilder, the more chance their client will walk.

A panel of qualified accountants and legal minds would take the lottery out of this decision-making process. I know that lawyers like that it is a lottery, but as a member of the public, if you have broken the law, you have been caught and you know you've done it, then why should it be such a lottery. An academic game played by legal experts at the expense of ordinary people.

The other offence is Rape. Why would this be? Surely this is a straight-forward concept, easily grasped by normal people. Well, yes and no. It is not so much a problem of whether or not jurors can grasp the concept, more a case of whether they are willing so to do. As I mentioned earlier, I would make sure I was involved in all the decision-making processes throughout the course of any investigation, right up to and including the trial. To that end, I attended every meeting and was there throughout the trial wherever possible. I took an interest in the selection of the jury as well. I had no control over the selection process – it is random, no one has control. Too many women on a jury trying a rape case was never good. I always felt that the defendant was going to get away with it. Not sure why. I am sure psychologists could wax lyrical about the subject ad infinitum. My colleagues, most of whom were women, just thought that women tend to be more judgemental with members of their own gender.

It Is also an irrefutable fact that if more than three people on a jury will not agree with the rest, then the whole trial is abandoned. When it comes to rape trials, there are many people out there who just don't recognise that rape is a thing. Some just think that women should just do as they are told. Some believe that a married woman has no say in the matter and the husband has rights over her. There are also people from other cultures who feel that the woman is always at fault, and the man should never be found guilty. In this country, the age of consent is 16. Under this age, you are not legally able to consent, and another person is not allowed to seek it. There is a section within the act that says that under the age of 12, you do not have the capacity to understand what you are consenting to. This leaves a grey area of between 12 and 16 but the fact is that the age of legal consent in the UK is 16. In some countries, it is 12. There are other countries where it is believed that any time after puberty – whenever that may happen – is the age at which people can consent. This is fine in itself. The problem comes when someone from one of those cultures is sitting on a jury in the UK. Even British citizens whose family come from elsewhere in the world have this issue. Some will take these cultural discrepancies and apply it to the law of this country. They don't care what the law of this land says. People are inherently immovable when it comes to their default cultural beliefs. This means that if there are three people with beliefs that contradict the principles of our legal system sitting on a jury, you have probably lost your case.

A woman walked into her front room to find her 40-year-old brother having penetrative sex with her 9-year-old daughter. Bearing in mind my previous comments about ages, now add the other aspect into the mix. While a person under 12 cannot consent, a person over 21 is duty-bound to ascertain the true age of those they have sexual encounters with. This means he cannot claim that he thought she was older. The law does not allow for that. Not that this case is fraught with those issues. An uncle would surely know. So, an investigation was conducted. Statements were taken, he was arrested and interviewed. His DNA was extracted from samples taken from the child. The investigation was able to confirm ages. The mother provided an eyewitness. Almost unheard of in rape cases. He was charged and went to court. The investigating officer had never had such a water-tight case. Despite this, after a week of evidence, the jury couldn't come to a decision. It was a hung jury and the trial was abandoned. The only explanation that I could come to was that more than 3 and less than 9 people did not believe that an offence had been committed. They could not have believed that the incident didn't happen. There was far too much evidence for that, so they must have taken the view that the girl was complicit and that made it all fine.

Fortunately, the CPS insisted on a retrial with a fresh jury and justice was eventually done... but it goes to show. This doesn't happen in other types of cases. Yes, you will get the odd idiot who decides that because he doesn't like police, he's going to give 'not guilty' decisions for everything thinking that he is getting to the police. These people aren't thinking of the community into which they are allowing these criminals, but that is relatively rare. Sadly, it is not rare in rape cases.

A panel of jurors who are vetted for their views, and are known to make decisions based on the law of the land and not some misguided belief in what they think the law should be, would level the playing field somewhat. I'm not suggesting a panel of compliant people who will be easily bullied into making decisions. I am suggesting a group of people who understand the evidential standards and will make decisions based on that.

Jury Monitoring

While we are being controversial, let's try this on for size. Recording all jury discussions. It has long been a staple of our law, that cases should only be discussed by jurors when they are all present together. This discussion is private and for their ears only. Not even the judge is allowed to know what they discuss. I have sat on two juries in my life, so I have an idea of what they like to discuss and what they bring to the table. There are people out there who don't care a jot about the law and will try to bring juries around to their way of thinking. In one of my juries, one of my fellow jurors didn't want to convict in a case that had been so obviously proven beyond all doubt, because he didn't like the victim. Sod the law, "I don't like the victim, and the suspect is a good-looking young lady." He didn't succeed in this case because he couldn't get around the evidence. You also have the rape issues that I mentioned in the previous subject and many other things that just get shoved under the carpet. If these discussions could be recorded, the recording then sealed and kept under lock and key so that if it is discovered that something illegal happened, (like jury nobbling or even if a clear case goes the other way contrary to all common sense), then it can be properly investigated by properly appointed legal minds.

Without knowing what was said, even if we know something illegal has happened, no one will ever know the truth. It would also make people think twice about turning juries away from obviously correct decisions.

This will never happen, there isn't a politician in the country who has the cahoolies to make that sort of decision.

Most of us are aware of the 'beyond reasonable doubt' thing that the courts used. What people may not know is that this has been disregarded in favour of a different phrase. They felt that it was beyond the ken of the average juror to suss out what 'reasonable' was and felt that what is reasonable for one person, may not be for another. Instead, they went with the phraseology 'so that you are sure'. This, in my view, is very airy-fairy and causes just as much confusion. Taken to the logical conclusion, no juror will know for absolute certain what has happened because they weren't there. If they were there, then they shouldn't be on the jury. Jurors often feel that this standard is so severe that you would have to have been there in order to be able to give a guilty verdict. In my jury experiences, I have felt no confusion. The evidence was there, the evidence was irrefutable. Guilty. All the defendant has to do is come up with any old rubbish and the jury are thrown into confusion. They are allowed to believe a load of rubbish if the defendant says it, but they have to question even the most reasonable accounts if it comes from a victim or witness.

What most people may not be aware of on this subject, is that, although the defence need to prove nothing whatsoever, if they were to provide evidence, the standard of proof is much lower. A defendant need only show that, on a balance of probabilities, what they say could have happened. Not what I would call a level playing field but, hey, no one ever said life should be fair. What does happen, unsurprisingly is that the jurors also take a much more liberal view.

A man is arrested having been caught stealing a tie from Harrods during their Winter Sale. The time of year is significant. It is winter and it is 4pm. It is therefore dark outside. He went to court and told the judge that he did not try to steal the tie. He was merely going outside the store to see if the tie matched his shirt in natural light, not the artificial Harrods lighting. I will leave it to the readers to decide if this was, on a balance of probabilities, a reasonable defence given the time of day and the ambient light outside the store. Suffice to say, the Judge thought it perfectly reasonable and acquitted him.

A young lady of about 18 makes an allegation of rape against a boy of around the same age with whom she had a relationship. She had some mild mental difficulties, as did he. Not so bad that they couldn't hold down jobs, but quite obvious when spoken to. When the boy was arrested, he said to the arresting officer after he was cautioned, "I'm sorry, I shouldn't have raped her." This was completely unsolicited and was recorded at the time. He and his solicitor were shown the note in the ensuing interview and agreed that he stated those words. Everything was properly recorded, handled and disclosed at the proper times and correctly handled. He was charged and went to court. In court, in the absence of the jury, the defence argued that the admission evidence should be removed as it was prejudicial to the defendant. The Judge, in making his decision, confirmed that the admission was indeed unsolicited. He stated that it was correctly recorded, disclosed and handled throughout the entire investigative process. He then said that the evidence could not be used as it was damaging to the defence. Well... yes! It's supposed to be. That is what evidence is. Imagine if all evidence was removed for this reason. That would be fun! Just imagine, "Officer, you know that evidence that you have that proves your case beyond all doubt? Well, you can't use it because it proves your case beyond all doubt." Sounds perfectly okay.

Now, because they both had mild mental problems, and the victim had not covered herself in glory in the run-up to the trial, the boy was acquitted. I think the judge felt, as I did, that this evidence would be damning. He would be found guilty and the judge would have no choice but to hand down a custodial sentence. The judge, in my view quite correctly, decided that prison was not the place for this unfortunate young man so he deliberately removed the evidence in the hope that the jury would acquit. I don't believe that the decision was correct, but I believe it came from the right place. He wasn't dangerous, and I don't believe he will go on to do anything similar.

Police

If you have read this far, it may not surprise you that I have an opinion. Whether you agree or disagree with me, those opinions are not set in stone. If someone comes to me with a good argument, I have no problem holding my hands up and conceding. It must be said that most of my opinions are borne of experience and not just what I have read somewhere. I am an avid reader. I take much of my knowledge, such as it is, from reading, but opinions are created through the combination of knowledge gained by reading and experience. So, when it comes to the Metropolitan Police Farce I think my opinions are well grounded.

It is my opinion, for example, that the best coppers – be they detectives or uniformed officers – could have fallen on either side of the legal divide as youngsters. Many a time I have watched in awe as a colleague has seen a situation, made an assessment and sussed the whole scenario in seconds. It always seemed to me that they understood the sort of people we were dealing with at a much deeper level than I did. I grew up in colonial Africa. I was surrounded by colonial people who all thought the same thoughts, did the same deeds and drank the same wine. I understand (and therefore don't particularly like) the colonial stereotype. I, therefore, think that some of my colleagues had a similar relationship with the criminal world. They seemed to think in the same way, they just tended to lean towards the right side. I don't know that this is true, but it fits.

Community Policing

Where do I start? Well, at the beginning, I suppose. When I joined the Met Police, there was 27,000 of us. The establishment was in the middle of being increased to around 30,000. There was a handful of civilian staff in each station. They were there to deal with post, pay and other admin-type jobs. There was a police station in each area which included a home beat officer for each ward. They dealt with community issues and went out to engage with the public. There was a Criminal Investigation Department (CID) to carry out the more serious investigations. Uniformed officers walked the streets and drove 'panda' cars. They dealt with the day-to-day policing demands. They spoke to people, they stopped shady looking people, they investigated minor crimes and hassled villains. If you found property, you'd take it to the local station. If no one claimed it within 28 days, you would have two weeks to claim it for yourself. If you found a dog, the local station would take care of it until Battersea Dog's Home came to collect it. If someone claimed it before they arrived, the police would ask for a small donation to the widows and orphans fund. If you had been the victim of a crime, you went to your local station and reported it. Even the Computer Aided Despatch (CAD) room, where calls are taken and jobs assigned to police officers out on the street, was staffed by police officers who had a good local knowledge of the area they were in, and luckily knew something of the law. This meant that good quality advice would quite often suffice, and the officers on the street wouldn't be despatched to calls that police should not have to deal with.

Now, I am not suggesting that these were halcyon days where everyone respected the local police, and kids got a clip round the ear and returned to their parents for another one if they were being naughty (or sometimes just for getting caught). What I am saying is that it was better than what we have now in many ways.

There are now 32,000 police in the Met, thousands of Community support officers or PCSOs (CHIMPS were the unkind but not entirely unwarranted phrase used by some. It was an acronym for Can't Help In Most Police Situations). We also have tens of thousands of civilian staff. There is a whole department dealing just with filing case papers and sending them to the CPS clerks who file them in another building. The Chief Superintendent has an entire office of staff to deal with their wants and needs. Interestingly, the population of London has increased by about 20% in the last 35 years, yet the police family has increased by something in the order of 50-60%. This was all to allow warranted police officers to get out from under the pile of unneeded paperwork, and onto the streets where they could do some good. Of course, all the paperwork generated by this meant that the pile of unneeded paperwork just got bigger. Officers then had to spend even more time stuck in police stations trying to dig their way out of it.

In the meantime, they have closed most police stations, so no one has a local any more. The police don't deal with lost property any more. Nor do they don't deal with stray dogs, we are encouraged to report crimes online, so they report fewer crimes in person. No one sees police officers walking around, chatting to the public. They are all in cars buzzing around chasing after the next stat that their inspector needs. We only see police officers if we are being arrested or are the victim of some crime that a politician has decided is a high priority at that point in time and requires a personal touch. When I transferred out of my first station, one of the local shopkeepers came to my leaving party. I bet no one can say that these days.

Police stations are now full of detectives dealing with all crimes, from the minor neighbour quarrel right the way up the scale. They are buried under a huge pile of paperwork from which they may never emerge. We have uniformed police officers who do little more than report crimes, attend burglar alarms or pub fights all to collect their inevitable statistics. They never investigate crime; they just report it and pass it along to the CID. This means they never learn what is required to complete a forensic investigation. They never understand the evidential trail that is required to take a case through court. This means that statements and scene management are not understood, and evidence is often lost as a result. We have a department that was created specifically for the community, staffed by a sergeant, two constables and a bunch of PCSOs and volunteers. It was supposed to replace the old 'home-beat officers. This entire department is there to appease politicians, not to get to know the community. I may spot a member of the police family out and about... once a year at most. They don't engage with the public. The public do not know their local officers other than through social media. Adding to this, of course, the CAD room is no longer local and no longer staffed by police officers. This means that when you call the police, you get someone with no local knowledge, and worse, no knowledge of police powers and procedures. This means that the police on the street get sent to everything that comes through the CAD room, regardless of its nature and relevance to the police.

The worst aspect of this policy is that police are distanced from the public. That means that they, the public, can't form personal opinions about the service or the officers involved. Following that, whatever the media or politicians choose to say about the police may well be believed. The public, after all, have nothing else to go on.

This, in my opinion, is the wrong way to police the capital. I have an idea of why this is happening. I have little to back it up in terms of merit but is based on cynicism bordering on conspiracy theory. I'll therefore leave the information there for the reader to decide.

Crime Prevention

The first duty of a police officer is to prevent crime. If despite their best efforts, they fail in this task, they have to then investigate the resulting crime and try to find justice. This sounds simple enough, but we are not only fighting criminals to achieve the primary function. We are also fighting politicians.

The problem is that crime prevention just isn't sexy. How many TV programmes are there on crime prevention? How many times do you switch on to watch your favourite TV cop drama to be told, "Sorry, no episode today, the police prevented the crime so there is nothing to show"? Perhaps then you should ask yourself how many people there are out there who would prefer not to be robbed in the first place, rather than having to go through all that investigative palaver and have some spotty oik sent to prison. No one gets their property back. No one really gains anything. Society as a whole may breathe a collective sigh of relief that the one robber that is caught is not going to be nicking their stuff for a couple of weeks, but that is about it.

Politicians are really not interested in it for other reasons. One of their main overriding concerns is that you can't measure success in this area. If you can't measure success, you can't tick a box. If you can't tick a box, well, what's the point of anything. Yes, we are always hearing that crime is up or down over the same period last year. We get those sorts of headlines in the news all the time. The thing is, none of those stats come as a result of crime prevention or lack thereof. They are just statistics being manipulated. Nothing more.

So, sorry folks, but the primary function of the police service of this country is just not sexy enough. As a young officer in Chelsea, a colleague and I set up an operation to try to detect the burgeoning Rolex watch robberies that were proliferating in the area. We found where most of it was happening and how it was happening. We set up a surveillance operation to try and catch them at it. Unfortunately, in those days, in order to set up surveillance, I had to tell everyone in the world what I was doing in case I was stepping on some other department's operational toes. The villains, therefore, got to know about it and disappeared the day the op started. We stuck it out for a week but found nothing other than a chemist who appeared to be flogging a lot of what we found out was illicit methadone to the local junkies.

What was noted during the week of the op, was that not a single Rolex watch robbery was reported in that area, and very few in the surrounding area. The number of robberies recorded in the following 6 months was very low. The miscreants who were doing the robbing were nowhere to be seen. When it came to reviewing the operation, it was deemed a failure as no intel came out of it and no one was arrested. When I mentioned the crime prevention aspect, the man was not interested as he didn't have a crime prevention box to tick and, in his words, "we can't measure the number of crimes prevented, only those detected".

Communication

I was a busy chap and always had a strong work ethic. It was because of that that I was able to learn how to deal with people. How to communicate and extract information. I was reminded as a young copper, that I had two eyes, two ears, and one mouth. If I used them in those proportions, it would be to my benefit. So, I did. I started out in Chelsea, which is an interesting place to learn the practicalities of policing. Most of the population were well-to-do 'old money', mixed with some new money and a load of successful artistic people. In this mile and a half square area was five council estates with everything that goes with council estate issues. So, I could be speaking to some Lord and Lady Muck one moment, then turn the corner and be dealing with drug-addled council estate youth. I would then be onto some airy-fairy head-in-the-clouds arty bloke. And you need to speak to them at their level. You can no more say, "Oy, mate, what's your game?" to Lord Cadogan than you could say, "Excuse me, sir, I wonder if you would be so good as to accompany me..." to some spotty council estate oik. You would get confusion in equal measure from both sides.

You do, of course, get the middle bit too. There was one particularly well-known, aristocratic ne'er-do-well in Chelsea who regularly bilked cabs because he had blown his frugal £10,000 weekly allowance on drugs and hookers. When he was sober, he was delightful, when he was on it, he was not. We felt quite comfortable speaking to him in whatever fashion we felt appropriate.

The trickiest thing a police officer has to do is maintain a balance. Not everyone can do it. Whoever you are conversing with when you are on official business, be they the Lord of the manor or the little tea leaf on the street, you had to maintain control of your environment and maintain a certain amount of authority. Not so much that you intimidate or belittle, but enough to allow you to do your job and walk away with whatever you needed. Not what they wanted. This often meant having to subtly raise your game if the other person was trying to get the better of you without them realising it. Everyone thinks they know better and as a result, say some pretty stupid things.

The Things People Say

It is human nature that we remember the bad things about people much more readily than the good. These pages are littered with references to people with whom I have not seen eye-to-eye. That being said, it is an organisation of 30,000 officers, so if I reference two or three people in a less than kind light. I have personally met over a thousand, so you will understand that the overwhelming majority are just doing their jobs and keeping their community as safe as their abilities will allow. Once the first flushes of inexperience have been washed away, you start realising that when people are shouting at you or insulting you, it is the uniform they are having a go at not you personally. Were you to walk down the street in plain clothes past a person who, an hour earlier, had berated you for some perceived indiscretion while you were in uniform, they would probably not even see nor much less recognise you.

Don't get me wrong, these people are trying to be personally insulting to the uniform. However, if it just all bounces off, try as they might, they can't succeed. But they do say some stupid things. I've had a 17-year-old say, "I know where you live!" as he was sent down to youth detention. Yawn. I can't tell you how many times I've also heard the phrase, "I'll have your badge for this!". Of course, they never did. There's also the classic, "do you know who I am?!" which often elicits ribald comments under the breath.

One young drunk with the silver-spoon-still-sticking-out-of-his-mouth was whisked in for being an utter prat one Friday evening, just outside a well-known Chelsea pub. In the back of the van heading towards the police station, he said, "wait until my father hears about this!" I replied, "Oh yes, as you are 15, I will need to speak to him. If you have his number, I would be grateful if you would give it to me." His bravado seemed to suddenly dessert him at that moment. He wasn't the big boy after all. The parents did come and collect him in the morning. They were mortified by their son's actions and were extremely apologetic. He was remarkably quiet as he slinked out of the station. Most of those types were very polite and decent once the alcohol and drugs wore off.

Then, of course, you had the woman who made an allegation of the robbery her Rolex watch and insisted that she was actually wearing two Rolex watches at the time. She claimed that both had been stolen. Doubtless, she also tried that one on the insurance company.

I once received credible evidence that a disgruntled retired public servant was going to use his retirement commutation to pay for a person to put me and a colleague into a compromising position enough to get us fired. He didn't mind whether it was drugs or prostitutes, as long as the colleague and I lost our jobs. The police actually went as far as putting an under-cover agent onto him to get to the bottom of it. He was quite serious. Unfortunately, he also had a quite serious drug problem. He blew his money before he could actually do the deal. No sleepless nights for me, of course. Prostitutes and drugs were never my thing. He was always going to fail.

How often have we heard "Police are all the same"? When I joined in 1987, it was a time when anyone who had a degree was considered very intelligent. Today, it seems, you need a degree to tie your own shoelaces, but then, it was only the academically advanced people who went to university. The Met Police at that time had more graduates than any other organisation in the country. At the same time in my class at the training college alone, there was a diverse group of people. One student came from a family of criminals. He hated his family with a passion. There was one guy who, I am told, was fired as he was running prostitutes. They found out that he was doing this when he first joined. The police service was like a second career for him. We had ex-military, ex-bankers and people straight from school all in the same class of 20 students.

We also hear some little burglar-type youngsters saying, "I can smell a copper from a mile off." Two points here, they never spotted me. One or two of these young villains have even said as much to me. I believe it was something to do with what I wore (I apparently didn't wear the jeans, open-collared shirt and Barber jacket that all the other police wore so I didn't stand out). Secondly, I believe many can spot us in a crowd. I say this because I could spot a criminal in a crowd. Not as well as some, but I could. If I can do that to them, why shouldn't it work both ways?

Rank

I never took promotion. When I became a detective, felt that I was in the right place. I took the promotion exam a couple of times and always passed the written tests. I just found it impossible to do the bullshit that was required to get through the scenario-based practical tests. I also came to the inescapable conclusion, that senior officers were no longer looking for leaders. The police service is a practical profession. You only learn it by doing it. What you first learn is to control your environment and maintain control of situations. Those who take promotion are essentially taking on a position that needs to control the controllers. For this, you do not need managers, you need leaders.

The senior officers wanted Inspectors who do as they were told and make sure their statistics showed the senior management in a good light. Beyond that, they could not care less. They received a load of training in handling the press, saying the right things at the right time, being 'all things to all men' (well, to the senior management). Any sign that you were there on behalf of the people you were supposedly leading was deemed an issue. Some would-be managers seemed to think that they needed to show their mettle by disciplining some unfortunate PC. To them, it was a tick in some little box somewhere on their computer screen. No one ever considered that if a situation has got as far as discipline, then you, as a leader, have already lost the battle because your troops aren't listening to you.

I don't think I could have been a part of that toxic atmosphere. I made sure I never became some up-and-coming DI's pet project. I just did what I did in my way and challenged them to find a more effective way by delivering results. They never could so I was left alone for the most part.

When I did 'act up' in the next rank in the absence of the regular DSs, I found it quite straight forward. By then, I had the confidence of my colleagues. I never really had to demand anything. One has to be careful when acting up because, at some point, you will be back at your own rank and at the mercy of your peers. I didn't have this issue. It seemed to me, that a suggestion was enough to convince people it was the right road down which to go. I may not have been Mr Dynamic DS, but I don't think I would have pulled that off anyway. I led; I didn't manage.

In terms of the other ranks, I had a stormy relationship with half and a very civil one with the other. I have had DCIs with whom I could barely speak because they were clueless. Some insisted on proving how clueless they were by sticking their oar in constantly. Some would just hide under the desk and avoid all confrontation. The ones I got on well with were the ones with whom I had very little in the way of personal contact. They were the ones that trusted their DIs and gave us space to do our jobs. I would only have personal contact with them when I was in trouble. If they allowed me to work, I didn't get into trouble. Most of the DIs with whom I had issues, were the ones who didn't trust their staff and didn't allow us to do our jobs. Those that thought that because they were a DI, they knew more than I. They wouldn't believe a word I said unless a DS confirmed it. Of course, the DS would get all their information from me anyway. These DIs were painfully clueless.

Working in the sexual offences unit, I had a DI with whom I had respect. Through the course of a year, I had about a dozen cases going to court. All but one were successful. I worked well with everyone in my team but seemed to click with one or two people in particular. We knew how each other worked. We enjoyed many successes. Then the DI left initiating a number of interdepartmental moves. I ended up with a DI who had a history of struggling to assert her authority due to her almost total lack of self-esteem. She surrounded herself with two DSs and refused to allow anyone to make any kind of decision outside that little triumvirate. So if a job came in, the DI and the two DSs disappeared into a locked office for two hours. They would then emerge having solved the entire case... at least in their heads. They then assigned someone as the 'investigating officer'. This was so that the report had someone else's name on it. This was handy for them because if the case went wrong, they had someone else to blame. They then assigned everyone a task, most of which were pointless, and wasn't interested in any discussion. We would have office meetings which were prefaced by her saying something like, "This is my meeting, you are here to listen, not talk". During that year, I was stopped from working with the ones with whom I had enjoyed the majority of my successes. While I was in that environment, I only had two 'successful' investigations. One was taken off me on the day I was going to charge the suspect and given to one of her pets. That job was dropped before it got anywhere near a court. The other was an inherited case that failed at court. My efficacy went from a dozen cases with 11 convictions in a year to zero. The other DIs were fully aware of the issues and were keeping a 'listening watch'. When it eventually came to a head, I was approached by one of the other DIs. He assured me that moves were afoot to resolve matters in my favour although I was to say nothing about it to anyone. I was moved out of that team onto a different team under that DI. The next year, having returned to my own ways but not with the colleagues I liked to work with, I had 7 successful investigations 5 of which were successful at court. Several others were looking sound before I handed them on when I retired. Could be a coincidence.

Police vs public

Many people think that if they get into a scrape with the police, they are going to come down on them hard. They believe that if they are in an accident on the road involving a police vehicle, the police will have their license away and do you for all sorts of weird RTA offences. Nothing could be further from the truth. I took a standard response driving course which allowed me to tear around the streets at break-neck speeds getting to the scenes of desperate incidents like a cat up a tree or someone locked out of their house. I stopped doing this after 5 or 6 years because I realised that I was being told to get to scenes as quickly as possible but if I then made a mistake, I would be risking my personal civilian license, and sometimes even my freedom. The police had no compunction to send police drivers to court and have their DVLA driver's license off them even if it was not really their fault. If you are driving above the speed limit, you are responsible and have to drive accordingly. If you take too long to get there, you are putting people's lives at risk. They had a tick-box that said I had to be at an incident within a certain amount of time. If I didn't get there, I failed. And then the inspector didn't get his next rank. Very important, that. There was no give in the system. I even got a parking ticket when parking an unmarked police car at an unused bus stop that all the marked police cars used when they were on their break. I wasn't even on my break, I was working, but I still had to pay the ticket.

So no, you won't be persecuted by police for getting into an accident with them. If anything, it was the other way around. I gave up driving those cars until they decided that they would support their officers in cases where they weren't being reckless. It never happened. Their attitude was that they were doing me a favour by allowing me to drive their cars, so I never drove marked police cars again. With favours like that, I'll take the alternative every day of the week and twice on Sundays.

Picture this – a marked police car on an emergency call. Blue light going, siren blaring, the full Monty. The police car was approaching a traffic light junction. The traffic was not very heavy for London. It is relatively free-flowing. The lights were green in his favour. He was going straight and the cars on either side to the left and right were stationary. The only other car of significance was a black cab that was moving into the junction from the opposite direction. Without warning, the cab then performed a U-turn within the traffic-light-controlled junction, straight into the path of the blaring, flashing, brightly coloured, speeding police car. As this is London, the police car wasn't going hell for leather, but he wasn't crawling either and had nowhere to go other than into the side of the cab. No one was prosecuted on this occasion, but the investigation was hellbent on finding fault with the police driver. Taxi drivers insist that, as their cabs are designed with a very tight turning circle, they are allowed to perform U-turns wherever and whenever they want. I wonder if that is the same for the driver of a Ferrari. A car that is designed to go at 180 miles an hour. Would they be allowed to scoot down Chelsea Embankment at full-tilt because their vehicle is designed to do that? I think not.

Cabs doing U-turns are a regular thing I had to deal with it all the time. I once came across a contretemps in the middle of the six-lane carriageway of the A4, near the V&A museum. A car came close to collecting a cab doing a U-turn on that road and lost his rag. I didn't blame him. The cab driver just said, "It's a cab. It's designed to do U-turns". Yes, but not on one of the busiest sections of one of the busiest roads in London at 11pm when the traffic is constant but light enough to be going at the speed limit. That is just stupid. An articulated lorry could perform a U-turn in that road if it needed to because it is that wide so 'tight turning circles' are somewhat redundant. I let him know my feelings on the subject. It didn't enter his thick skull.

Arrest notes

The writing of arrest notes became a real issue the more human rights and transparency prevailed. When I joined, the Arrests notes were just that – notes. They were abbreviated, they gave the facts and nothing else. If a formal statement was required, it was written with the arrest notes as an exhibit, but they were the officers' notes. They were written on a small A6-sized booklet. They showed the date, time, and place as well as explaining the incident in two or three words. For example, 'Arrest – assault' or 'Domestic incident'. The next page showed who the main parties were and all their known details. There was then a further section to record descriptions and a further one for recording property. Then came the 'Evidence' pages. This was where you wrote down what had happened. Back in the '80s and '90s, this was in note form including the abbreviations and such like. At the end was a record of charges. I heard of one particular officer who walked into court to give evidence in a case of Drunk and Disorderly. The front page was completed properly, as was the page where details of persons involved were recorded. All other pages were also properly completed. The evidence page was brief. All it said was "NEDD." Nothing else. This was perfectly acceptable. The officer would simply read the details of the date, time and place that were recorded on the front. He would then turn to the next page and supply the person's details. The rest was just the evidence required to prove drunk and disorderly. 'Normal Evidence, Drunk and Disorderly'. This was pretty generic – "his eyes were glazed, his breath smelt of intoxicating liquor, he was unsteady on his feet and he was verbally abusive to passers-by. He continued in this manner even when I approached him to tell him to desist. In my opinion, he was drunk". This was the only offence in which the police could give an opinion. They were considered experts in drunkenness. Knowing some, I could see why.

Police then started being asked about all sorts of other stuff like what force was used, whether it was appropriate and justified, what was said, how it was said and to whom. So, a rethink was required. Those reports could no longer be brief arrest notes but had to include everything. Self-defence training started to include lessons about what should be included in arrest notes. What was said, what was done and what force was used. What we ended up with, was reams upon reams of how the handcuffs were applied, why they were needed, what alternatives were thought of and rejected, and why. Precise wordings of conversations had to be dealt with. After I had read War and Peace about all this stuff, the officer would then put in a line about what the unlucky chap was arrested for and what the grounds were. Sadly, there were occasions that even this was completely forgotten about. I would read about how wonderful the officer safety module was being observed but nothing about why the arrest was made in the first place nor what the grounds for arrest were.

Quite an important piece of information one would think. I would suggest, somewhat more important than the manner in which handcuffs were applied.

I seldom used handcuffs. There were occasions where I would be at someone's house making an arrest and I would say to them that I had no desire to embarrass them in front of the neighbours. Our car was unmarked and he could walk out with us without handcuffs. I did have a situation where I told the suspect that if they did have a mind to run off, he was probably a much faster runner than I was so I would not give chase. I would, however, find him again and would have no compunction in embarrassing him in front of his neighbours on that occasion. It did the trick.

The Burden of Proof

It has been said that we would prefer to let 10 guilty people go free than convict one innocent person. This is rather glib and very easy to say. Just remember, the police and the lawyers, in the overwhelming majority of cases, weren't there when the incident they are grappling with occurred. They only have an evidential trail. Much of that evidence is verbal and most people never tell the full story. I heard a barrister once say that with the number of hoops a police officer has to jump through just to get a case to court, it is highly unlikely that the defendant, in any case, is entirely innocent.

Let me clarify this. We'll take a random generic case of assault. This is the process that we have to go through if it is going to get to a jury trial. We will take it that the allegation is true.

A person makes an allegation. It is investigated, injuries recorded by a doctor and the investigation completed. At some point during the process, the suspect is arrested. In order to have him booked into custody, the arresting officer has to convince a custody Sergeant of the evidence that exists, which provided grounds for the arrest. The Sergeant isn't involved in the arrest or the investigation. If the fact is that there aren't sufficient grounds, then the Sergeant gets into trouble if he authorises detention. He isn't going to risk his career, so you have to convince him. To keep the individual in custody for sufficient time to reasonably conduct your enquiries, the investigator has then to convince an inspector at regular intervals that the detainee's continued incarceration is required. The same applies to the inspector in terms of their involvement in the case and ongoing career prospects. Then, in order to take the case further, the investigator has to convince the DI that there is sufficient evidence to take it to the CPS. Now, while the DI wants the charge to go through because it makes his figures look good, he doesn't want to get it in the neck by the CPS. He has to be satisfied that all the ducks are in a row and everything that can be done has been done before he will give his authorisation for the case is sent to the CPS. The investigator puts the file together for the CPS rep to peruse. The CPS, as has been discussed previously, will not authorise a charge unless they have no choice. They will fight tooth and nail to not charge someone and only weight of evidence can convince them otherwise. They have their stats to worry about.

A charge is authorised, and the defendant is sent to the magistrates' court. A trial by jury then needs to be decided upon. The magistrates have to be satisfied that there is sufficient evidence for this to go ahead. They do not want to waste valuable court time on something that will fail.

The man is 'sent down the road' in police parlance to face a jury of his peers. The crown court will periodically review the case to make sure everyone is playing their part correctly. The defence, if they find the smallest chink, will try to get the case dropped at every turn. The judge will have all the paperwork and will know how much of a chance the case has. If he doesn't have confidence in the case, he will be more sympathetic to the defence. If he thinks the case is strong, he will often lean towards the prosecution. This is not always how it works, but it does happen regularly.

The trial then starts and a jury is empanelled. They hear the evidence the court allows them to hear. They have no idea of all this process that has gone before. Convincing sceptical Sergeants, sceptical CPS, sceptical defence lawyers.

It seems that it is genuinely thought by some people that the police will decide someone is guilty and then drag them kicking and screaming into court to get his comeuppance. Nothing could be further from the truth. If there is insufficient evidence, it would be picked up by the investigating officer. The CPS would never see it. This is because a case is often dropped before even reaching that stage. So, there you have it. Yes, it is important that innocent people aren't convicted. However, the likelihood of this occurring is, as you can see, insignificant.

Medals

I never sought glory. I wasn't interested in medals and, although it is always nice to be recognised by one's colleagues, I got more of a kick out of members of the public who showed appreciation for my work. I realised very early on that medals were there for political reasons only. It only recognised acts of officers going 'above and beyond' when it was of media or political advantage to the senior management. I also realised that when an officer walked straight past a sergeant or inspector to come and ask me for advice, the appreciation from my peers was much more important than some faceless commander or deputy assistant commissioner giving me a piece of paper to tell me that I had done my job to their satisfaction.

There are many examples of 'commissioner's commendations' going to admin staff for doing admin work while officers out on the street are facing unknown dangers at every turn. While I appreciate the work they do is required, they aren't putting their bodies on the line. Those that do are at the mercy of the subjective views of those who are handing them out. Essentially, if your boss doesn't like you, you don't get the recognition. That is, of course, unless he wants to get rid of you, then he may consider heaping praise on you so that any future application would be accepted by whichever department is considering him for transfer.

I have three examples that I hope will illustrate my displeasure with this system. I will go in chronological order.

Picture the scene. It's a night duty in Chelsea. It is midweek and in the small hours of the morning. Our hero is riding 'shotgun' (armed with his trusty truncheon – not a shotgun) in a marked police car with a colleague that he did not get along with (Previously described hereinabove as looking similar to Ian Hislop of Private Eye fame). A call to Kings Road is received. A woman has claimed that a man has threatened her with a firearm. Now, this is highly unusual. It's probably the first time the officer has been called to an incident involving weaponry like this. Over the police, personal radios, it was made clear that there were units nearby who would speak to the woman. These two officers would search the immediate area to try to find the miscreant. Another communication over the radio a short while later, confirmed that another unit had stopped a man nearby. As a result of this, the driver of the car stopped looking and mentally turned off. They were just entering the King's

Road, about half a mile from the incident, when a male that matched the description of the attacker was spotted. At the speed he was walking, this put him at about the right place at the right time, so our hero said to his colleague, "that's him, over there." "What are you talking about!" the driver's colleague retorts, "he has been stopped already." "No," the officer responds, "they have the wrong guy, that's him there." He then finally switched back on and looked to where the man was walking. Forming the same conclusion as his colleague, he drove up to the man and, as his partner was about to jump out, the driver said, "He's mine, don't arrest him." This didn't get a response. The officer got out of the car immediately behind the man. He grabbed the holdall the man was carrying so that any weapons he may have been carrying could be secured. He was arrested and handcuffed. The bag was searched and a firearm was found. The firearms team were called and the weapon proved. It was found to be a harmless but authentic-looking imitation. He was charged with possession of an offensive weapon. Nothing more was said. It was a low-level crime and nothing to write home about. A week later, back on day shift, an armed bank robbery occurred on the King's Road. Another officer literally bumped into a man as he ran out of the bank that he had just tried to rob, before the alarm was even raised. The bag he was carrying was dropped on impact, thereby disarming him before the officer knew what was happening. It turned out that he was also carrying an imitation firearm. Because this man was charged with armed robbery, the officer was given a commendation. Right place, right time and all the luck in the world. While the officer in the first scenario didn't do much that was worthy of any special recognition, he did approach a man who he suspected carried a firearm and disarmed him. My colleague in the second scenario did not knowingly confront that danger. I, therefore, believed that he was even less worthy. He only received it because of the level of the offence charged and the fact that the management liked him.

The second example really got to me. This was the tragedy that was the huge tsunami around India and surrounding countries in 2004. Few people are aware that a contingent of British police officers were sent out to assist in the recovery and identification of dead bodies. This was a terrible job carried out by constables, sergeants and a few inspectors. One of my close colleagues was amongst these people. He described scenes of utter devastation. Every day bought dead bodies, some starting to decay. It also brought distraught families, intense heat and misery.

They worked 15 hour days with little in the way of days off at weekends. About a week into the operation, a chief superintendent was despatched from London to oversee the operation. He remained in his air-conditioned hotel room and did the meeting-and-greeting with officials. He never met any of the officers, never spoke directly to anyone directly involved in the process and certainly never got his hands dirty dealing with dead bodies and grieving families. On return to England, a report was sent to the Home Office requesting that all officers be recognised for their tireless and distressing work. It was decided that the Chief Superintendent would receive a commendation but no one else. After all, the officers were just doing what they were paid to do. It was felt that this commendation was sufficient to recognise everyone's work. What we have here, is someone who did nothing of any value, taking on and being able to cite a commendation in his future promotion applications, while everyone else got nothing. This was not fair

My third was an incident that concerned football hooligans running riot on Croydon circa 2010. I was night duty CID and got on duty as the disturbances were just starting up. At least one of my night duty CID colleagues was caught in the middle of it all and was engaged in fighting back the crowds. This was made slightly more dangerous by the fact that he wasn't wearing a uniform and was therefore indistinguishable from the rioters. Many officers showed extreme bravery during that night. I was away from it all but was kept busy processing detainees and co-ordinating the gathering of intelligence. I was doing admin. The next week, everyone involved in the incident was given a superintendent's commendations. I was sent a message that there would be a short ceremony to recognise the work that the officers had done and that I would be receiving the same award. I didn't show up and, despite efforts from management to get me to go and collect it, I didn't go. I felt that my job was not worthy of special recognition. I was tucked safely away in the station. I was not putting my body on the line and I felt that awarding me diminished the efforts and bravery showed by those who did. Some of those officers worked a 16-hour shift. They were physically and mentally exhausted at the end. I worked a normal eight-hour shift. I may have done an extra hour or so to ensure the oncoming shift was aware of the issues but that was it. Nothing heroic. Nothing 'above and beyond', just a shift that was busier than normal. Certainly not in the same league as the others.

I do believe that workers respond positively to recognition. I understand the value of properly administered award systems. I also feel that politics should be kept out of it. Phrases like 'he was only doing his job' are unhelpful. If someone has done a good job, let that person know. It costs nothing but may encourage future good work.

Race relations

Now here is a subject that you can wrap your head around. Let me start with my personal beliefs. They are strongly held beliefs and, despite some attempts at persuading me otherwise, they remain intact. I personally do not care what colour your skin is, what god you pray to or from which country you or your ancestors come. If you are going to be my friend, it is because you are the sort of person I can relate to, what goes on inside your head and how you think. None of these things are affected by how dark your skin is. I believe that, if we all stop trying to find differences in people based on race alone, eventually we will forget that there are different races. If you want to look for differences in humans, I can name a few. You have tall people, short people, people with different colour hair. People who can add numbers quicker than others. People who can remember stuff. People who can recall and assimilate information. Some people are good with their hands, some are artistic and some are musical. There are loads of differences that we can all appreciate. They make the world in which live a more vibrant place. The one thing that makes not a jot of difference to anything is what colour your skin happens to be. It does not mean that you think any clearer or are better or worse than anyone because of it. It points to what the origins of your family may have been, but again, what difference does that make.

It was Mr Mandela who once said, *"Our world is not divided by race, colour, gender or religion. Our world is divided into wise people and fools. And fools divide themselves by race, colour, gender or religion."*

There is an issue of culture. A consequence of how people from different places have slightly different ways of thinking. Quite often, this is a religious thing, but I fear that all it does highlight the idea that there are differences. All the time we are being made aware of these differences, it reinforces the questionable belief that we are intrinsically different. Where this happens, it opens the door to allowing, some people to believe that one system is better than the other and this, in turn, reinforces racist attitudes. The differences are cosmetic. I believe that playing them down is the easiest way of curing the world of this particular disease – racism.

I do not listen to the MOBOs. I have never taken an interest in the Asian radio or TV networks. I don't attend religious festivals. I do not choose who I meet and associate with based on anything other than whether they are compatible. I do not believe that racism is the preserve of the white people of our society. Racism is not racist; it affects all people equally, be they the victims or the perpetrators. I am fully aware of what was done to Africans during the slave trading years. It was terrible and should never be repeated, but here's a thing, It was no worse than what they did to the Irish men when they were 'indentured' into service in America. (Polite way of saying 'enslaved') or what happened to the Jewish people in Nazi Germany. They were enslaved and literally worked to death. What seems to me to have been overlooked is the vibrant slave trade that continues to this day. Believe me, the slave trade isn't racist. They will destroy anyone's lives no matter their racial origin. And we need to remember that the slave traders and owners came from across the racial divide.

I spent my early years between the ages of 8 and 22 in Africa. I spent time in South Africa in the late 1960s. Not a nice place to be. I spent most of my time in Africa in what was Rhodesia, soon to become Zimbabwe. During my time in Africa, there was one indisputable fact that I knew. Everyone in that part of Africa was racist to one degree or another. Black people didn't associate with whites or Asian. Asian people didn't meet socially with black or white people. White people didn't spend their time with black or Asian people. Mixed race people kept to themselves. Arabic nations and the far eastern peoples were few and far between. We all seemed to work together perfectly well, we just didn't spend quality time together. I returned to England in 1983 and was absorbed into the great cosmopolitan melting pot that is London. Here I re-educated myself in the ways of racial awareness and very quickly came to realise that we are all essentially the same. We have the same ambitions, wishes and desires. No difference at all, really.

So I do not do the things that separate us racially, as I believe that they proliferate the belief that we are in some way different. For no other reason than the colour of our skin. All the time that happens, some people are going to believe that they are in some way superior or better than others. If we concentrate on what makes us a part of the same species that all come from the same place ultimately, then we will all start truly believing that we are the same and the problems will eventually diminish. If we try to look for quick fixes, we end up with this unworkable system that we appear to have now. It is true that the younger the person in this country the less chance they are of harbouring racist views. It's simply because they have grown up with each other, unlike some older folk.

It has to be a slow burn, and it can only be achieved by changing attitudes. This takes time, but it works. If you aren't sure about this, I will give two entirely unrelated examples of attitudes being the driving force behind overall change:

The first is drink driving. In the 1970s and 80s, there was an attitude to drink driving where many people didn't like drunks getting behind the wheel, but no one got that hot under the collar about it. It was illegal at the time. You would lose your driver's license if you were caught by the police. But the general view was that the driver was a bit of a twit, nothing more. The law hasn't changed much in terms of how much it will allow. It was always two pints, give or take. Most people had no problems with someone going to the pub and driving home as long as they weren't drunk. A campaign was initiated by the government. What they were suggesting, was that that drink drivers were the cause of accidents in which people other than themselves were dying. It started slowly and built up over the years. We hear little of this campaign now. No change in the law came as a result. There were no changes in the way the law treats drink drivers. But the attitude among the public has undergone a sea change. It is no longer socially acceptable to drink-drive. A person known for drink driving is looked down upon. It has become an embarrassment to admit to it. The legal limit hasn't changed, but it seems to me that the general public finds anything more than a half-pint to be unacceptable. It is entirely about the attitude of the public, and this has built up over the years to almost take over from the law and stand in judgement of offenders. It has taken 40 to 50 years, but we are getting there.

The second is smoking. Tobacco, primarily – it seems to me that among many, cannabis is more acceptable. The law about who can and can't smoke cigarettes has barely changed for 60 years. Where we can smoke has changed a lot. But this has only been made possible by the general attitude toward smoking. In the 70s and 80s when I first entered the workplace, most people smoked. They would smoke anywhere and everywhere, and they would have a cavalier attitude to littering. Slowly over time, attitudes have changed. A campaign about health has been going on in the background for decades. Any medical condition would be a shoo-in for the campaigners. We have all heard that pretty much any disease is exacerbated by smoking. Now, smokers are almost social pariahs. They can't smoke anywhere other than in their own homes and outside. Most people don't even smoke in their own homes. They go outside to do it because of the foul smell. While it isn't considered unacceptable to smoke, it has become unacceptable to foul the air of non-smokers. It is entirely due to the slow-burn campaign winning over hearts and minds.

In this country, it is socially unacceptable to discriminate in any way on the grounds of race. I'm not talking about official stuff. It goes much deeper. People don't like any kind of thought that would suggest a racist attitude. Even racists don't admit it outright. Yes, there are laws, and yes, there are demonstrations about this. But these measures don't do much of anything. Being on a demo is just telling a load of people what they already know: We don't like racism. If we just maintained this attitude and didn't consider racial differences in any way, this attitude will come, and it will be more socially unacceptable to more and more people.

I do not believe that 'positive discrimination' is healthy. I am aware that some people are under-represented in some areas of society, but if we take people on merit, this should eventually disappear. Positive discrimination is, in fact, illegal in any case as it is racist. Putting the word positive in front of a negative aspect – discrimination – does not make it better. In Mathematics, the product of a negative value and a positive value is always going to be negative. It is the same in language. "I ain't dun nuffing" (two negatives) must mean I have done something (Positive). So positive discrimination based on race just means that the speaker is in favour of racism. If you discriminate in favour of someone on a racial basis, it is obvious that you must have discriminated against someone else on the same basis. My opinion.

Steven Lawrence

Moving on. I was never involved in the investigative process of this tragic incident. I do not know any of the investigators or the people involved in the incident. I have however spoken to people who were involved in the investigations, some more peripheral than others. I have also had conversations with people who lived locally and who knew what many of the issues were. I could not tell anyone with any confidence exactly what happened on that occasion. I would suggest only three people in the world can. There seemed to me, to be a general view outside of the official standpoints, that the police investigation was lacking in many ways. This was supported by the officers with whom I spoke. There was, however, a feeling that the police were not the only problem and the Lawrence family should be taking a close look at the way they handled the affair as well. I couldn't say either way, but I did find it odd that they took on a lawyer who was well known for taking on cases that the media were all over. They employed them before anyone knew anything about it. Why do victims need a lawyer? And why would the lawyer refuse access to the family to enable police to carry out their investigation? Surely, regardless of what they thought of the police before this incident, they would have wanted it investigated. Questions, I fear, that were never even considered in the subsequent enquiry.

What I do believe, rightly or wrongly, is that the enquiry the Home Office set up was politically controlled. Its ostensible aim was to investigate the investigation. I believe that the actual brief was to criticise the police, preferably on the basis of it being racist. This view was highlighted by a question that was asked of one detective during the examinations. I can't remember how this question put, but his answer made it clear that he did not discriminate in any way between different races and cultures. As far as he was concerned, everyone should be treated equally. Big mistake! The invective that came at him from both the enquiry and the media was immediate and devastating. "How dare he treat everyone equally. This can only mean that you do not respect different cultures and would therefore ride rough-shod over the sensibilities of cultural minorities", was the cry from all sides

It was a setup. It would not have mattered how the officer answered that question, he would have got it wrong. I can see no argument against treating everyone equally. It isn't like he was forcing a Jewish person to eat a bacon sandwich while he was being interviewed. I have no issues with accommodating peoples' cultural proclivities as long as they don't interfere with the investigation of as serious an offence as this. If you want to pray to your god at 3 minutes past 4 in the evening on the hard shoulder of the A3285 while the sun is partially hidden behind one of Tolkien's orcs then go for it. It doesn't bother me, as long as the investigation isn't adversely affected.

I also found it a pointless exercise to call up the people who were suspected of committing the crime and asking them if they were racist. For a start, no one in their right minds is going to answer that question honestly if they are. Secondly, what on earth has that got to do with how the police conducted the investigation. To me, it just showed that the aim of the enquiry was not what they said it was.

In the end, the enquiry could not accuse the police of being racist because they would have to prove that. As the police, as an organisation, is demonstrably not racist, they had to look elsewhere. They didn't feel that they could say that 'some police officers' were racist as they would have to qualify – if not quantify – that, and they would have found that a rather small minority held those views and not all of them were white Anglo-Saxon males. It would not have the impact they were looking for. So by extension, they couldn't say 'most police officers' were racist as it would simply be untrue. So they plumped for a political way out. They invented (or perhaps reinvented) a phrase that they could redefine and manipulate to their purposes. Institutional Racism. This did not mean that any individual was being accused nor was the organisation itself. It was just the way things had been done and the underlying unconscious attitudes that the organisation held.

The effect was exactly what they wanted. They knew that people would hear this phrase and filter out the word institutional. That way anyone could accuse the police of being racist without actually accusing them of being racist. The Schrodinger's Cat of the politically correct.

Even more so they could turn that on any organisation that they wanted to insult knowing that the organisation could do nothing about it. It is still happening to this day. The media regularly accuses whole organisations of racism where there is little or no evidence exists simply by prefixing it with 'institutional.'

All this being said, it did bring about some positive changes in attitudes and improvement in how we investigate all offences. Especially the more serious ones. Essentially what they did was to standardise procedures so that all serious offences were given proper attention.

Racially aggravated offences

This is a big bugbear of mine. There was a huge opportunity for our legislators to have an impact on offences that were aggravated or motivated by racism. In my view, they signally failed to do this.

A decision was made by our beloved legislators, that offences committed by people that were based on race should be dealt with appropriately. The colour of one's skin is not a choice. It doesn't determine anyone's ability or attitude and should be treated as an aggravating factor. All good so far.

113

What they did was to create a piece of legislation that could be tagged on the end of other offences, so adding the aggravating factor to those that were already established. What was intended, was to give courts the power to add an extra 2 years onto the end of any sentence that would have been passed down in the absence of the aggravating factors. Everyone is happy with this. No problems there? Of course, there is!

In practice, it has become almost unworkable. There are a few reasons.

The powers that be made it easier to prove the aggravating factor by saying that if anyone – even someone who is not involved and wasn't even there – believed that there was a racial element involved, then it was to be treated as such. Regardless of whether or not the person being accused had any of those thoughts, and regardless of any evidence to the contrary. I don't see that this is reasonable. If someone is a racist then deal with them. If they are not, why try to paint them as such just to appease some political activists. Racism is a deliberate, thought-out process. You can't be 'accidentally' racist. I know people would like us to believe otherwise, but you can't. I will deal with this in more depth later in the chapter.

The next issue was how the practitioners dealt with the legislation. We will use an allegation of assault as an example. The allegation is made, and the person making the allegation states that the attacker used racially inflammatory language before, during or after the attack. The perpetrator is duly captured and dragged kicking and screaming to the police station. Now, here is the issue. The assault is a given. We can prove this. The victim has injuries commensurate with the details of the allegation. The suspect has injuries to his knuckles and blood splatters that can be linked to the victim. So charging him with assault is straight forward and the court will have no difficulty in convicting him. The racial aspect is slightly less clear. It is one word against another. Unless the police can corroborate that aspect, they may fail at court. The problem is, that if police charged our miscreant with the racially aggravated offence, they have to prove both parts. If one part fails, it all fails. You can't go into court and say, "This bloke thumped that bloke. Here is all the evidence you need to prove that. Oh, and by the way, we think he might have been a bit racist while he was doing it. Can you please string him from the yardarm on that basis?" It doesn't work like that. We may be able to treat the incident differently during the investigation phase, but at court, they need evidence. So if the person is charged with the aggravated offence and the court can't be sure enough on the racial aspect, he walks. He gets away with assault altogether. What this means is the CPS are less likely to charge with the aggravated offence. Especially if the evidence for the primary offence is so strong. The same works in the other direction. You can show that the person is a rampant racist but can't evidence the assault, he walks without a stain on his character. Can that be right?

It would have been so much easier to word this differently to take away this issue. It is not without legal precedence to have an 'either/or' option. Or just simply split the trial into two. First, prove the assault. Once that is safely locked away, decide on any aggravating features. One wouldn't even have had to put this into legislation. They would just have needed to amend the judges sentencing guidelines to include aggravating features. Alternatively, the judge can direct a jury to decide on each aspect individually. It is what it is, we have to work with it. Even though it doesn't work well. It's what the law is all about, isn't it? It is an Ass!

The last issue regards the offences to which this piece of legislation can be attached. As it is an additional two years on any sentence passed down, the law states that you can't 'add' two years to a life sentence as that is already the maximum sentence allowed. Now this, on the surface seems sensible. But it isn't.

If someone was to burn down a house and didn't care if there is anyone in there. If it is found that he has done this because one or more occupants has a skin shade slightly darker than the arsonist approved of, he can't be charged with Racially aggravated Criminal Damage by arson with intent to endanger life, as this carries a life sentence. The fact that the person, even if he did receive that sentence, and that is by no means a given, would probably serve no more than 15 years if no one was injured, is entirely by the by. The court has no power to say, for example, that the arsonist is sentenced to Life, the person is to serve a minimum of 15 years before being released on license and on top of that, the person is to serve an additional 2 years for the aggravating features. If life meant life, I would have no issues, but it doesn't. That person would then be released, and police would have intel that stated 'Arsonist' but not 'racist'. So the police intelligence systems are deprived of vital information. Intelligence-led policing would suffer. If there were a spate of racially aggravated arsons, he could slip under that investigative radar.

So, in my opinion, this piece of legislation was drawn up to appease activists, not to deal with a problem. They could have differentiated between aggravated and motivated offences. A racially motivated one tends to suggest a degree of planning and intent. The aggravated offences could be something that came up during the incident that added a different element. It doesn't seem to me that this was even considered. Or if it was, it was rejected.

Accidental Racism

It is my view that if you are racist, it is because you either dislike people of different racial backgrounds or, even if you are ambivalent, are willing to treat them differently, like overlooking people for promotion at work, excluding people from places and events etc. It is a deliberate thought process. It is not accidental.

Many of our older folk are criticised for being 'casually racist' often for nothing more than using outdated language. If a little old lady is describing someone to police and says, "...he was a coloured gentleman..." this does not mean she is being racist, just old.

Very recently there was an incident amongst our esteemed politicians where one was accused of racism – and had to apologise – when in fact, she was just showing empathy towards a fellow female colleague.

The incident involved Amber Rudd, a white female Conservative politician and Diane Abbott, a black female Labour politician. The story told of an interview about online trolling. Amber Rudd had stated that it was a serious problem. On being prompted, she confirmed that she believed it worse for women and more so for 'coloured' women. This was pounced on by Diane Abbott for the 'inappropriate use of language' The media were all over it. Everyone spoke about the racist use of language by a senior cabinet minister, not the fact that there were utterly idiotic cowards out there, hiding behind the internet, trolling people for their own entertainment. The whole timbre of the conversation was Amber Rudd explaining the awful things that many women in the public eye, have to go through. Whether or not it is worse for black women is open for discussion. I suppose if these cowards are picking on random features to insult people rather than policies, then why not race? But what difference would be made by Amber Rudd using phrases such as 'lady-of-colour', or 'black women' over 'coloured people'. The effect is the same – there are still idiots out there trolling, and women, especially black women, are adversely affected. Amber Rudd was not being insensitive because of using out-of-date language, she was being sensitive because she was highlighting current issues suffered by her colleagues across the political and racial spectrum. Anyone who found it offensive has a problem themselves and appears to have no problem with internet trolling.

I think the problem is that white racists will use all these issues as a stick to beat those of us who don't like the judgemental nature of racists and racism. At the same time, it can be used by black and Asian racists to drive the rhetoric that everyone who isn't a part of their racial group are themselves racist. Neither is correct and normal people can drive this out by not rising to their bad politics.

I was explaining to a friend not so long ago about my upbringing. I wanted to put across to him that as an eight-year-old, one absorbs everything around them, including attitudes. So as a young person growing up in Africa in the late 60s and 70s, I was racist along with almost everyone I knew. It is not the mistakes one makes in life; it is how one resolves those mistakes and learns from them. His attitude was that I was 'brave' to admit this. This attitude is, in my opinion, an encapsulation of why we are not getting it right. If you are considered 'brave' to admit a mistake, it suggests that perhaps it is better not to. If we do not encourage people to admit mistakes, we cannot correct them. They will then proliferate.

What comes off the back of that is a subtle form of censorship in which views that other people may disagree with are not voiced. If you stop people having opinions contrary to your own, these people will not necessarily stop voicing them, they will just voice them in a targeted way. This will almost always be away from our dissenting voices. So the opinions will be out there but away from public platforms and in darker areas where the views are in the ears of people more vulnerable to adopting bad ideas. If we allow the conversation, then we can use intelligent argument to destroy bad ideas. We will never stop people having bad ideas, but we can prevent the results of those ideas spreading. Not by censorship or taking away platforms on which these people can spout their garbage, but by showing that there is a better way. We can't do that if we don't know what they are saying.

So bring on the right-wing extremists. How easy is it to destroy their arguments? We won't ever convince the speakers, but we may have a chance the listeners. Bring on the racists. Let them say what they want to say. Don't get angry, just use intelligence. We will win the day in the end. Don't discourage people from admitting things that you don't agree with. Allow the conversation. Put the alternative view, it will be fine. Consider the time when the BNP leader Griffiths was allowed on Question Time on the BBC during a political debate prior to a general election. People railed at this and complained bitterly that he was allowed a platform to put across his nasty politics. It should have been an opportunity to listen to his points of view and, in a controlled atmosphere, highlight the fact that his ideas were odious. They could then have put the alternative point across. What happened instead, was that the BBC panicked and made sure that everyone on the panel was some sort of ethnic, cultural or religious minority. When a question was asked, Griffiths would answer it in a way that he felt was appropriate. Then every other member of the panel completely ignored the question, turned the conversation to a subject that they wanted to have a rant about. As long as it included having a go at Griffiths. Not for the answer that he provided but for what they felt was the subtext. So the results were that we understood what Griffith's views were, and we understood that the other panellists didn't like Griffiths. What we didn't know, was what the opinions of the other panellists on the questions at hand were. It was an unfortunate victory for the BNP. The media the next day went on the offensive. They told everyone how Griffiths was destroyed in the debate. He wasn't. They didn't even come close. His supporters walked away believing that he had won the day. All it would have taken was for the panel to answer the questions. They would have prevailed. It wasn't difficult.

Sharia Law

I feel this subject needs to be covered briefly. There are those in this country who believe that Sharia Law is a confirmation of their culture and, as the laws of this country deal with things differently, they should be allowed to practice their version of the law. Firstly, I believe that the overwhelming majority of Sharia law encompasses the same subjects and restrictions as that of our laws. I am no expert so, if I get this wrong, I apologise. Those parts that don't are either insignificant or entirely contrary to the laws of this country. I am thinking of the way that sexual offences are dealt with and the way women, in general, are represented. There are also issues with regards to punishments. In those circumstances, many of the sections of the Sharia law are, in fact, illegal under our legal system, and so cannot be overlooked. I don't believe that there should be one law for one section of society and one for another. So I reject the calls for this law to be observed. It isn't like we can allow the parts that do comply with our law and ban the rest because then you may as well say that we have to observe our existing laws. I also feel that it encourages the 'them-and-us' culture, of which we so desperately need to rid ourselves.

A hypothesis

As a parting shot on this subject, I want to put a hypothesis. It has long been thought, that in the future with a much more liberal view of 'mixed marriages', that everyone will eventually be coffee-coloured. But consider this hypothetical scenario.

If it was decided, worldwide, that everyone would stop travelling abroad and no one ever left the country of their residence. Everyone carried on as we were but just never going abroad.

If at the same time, the climatic conditions of the earth remained similar to what it is now - with mild variations - but no real changes happening, (This is highly unlikely but that's why it's hypothetical) what would we all look like after, say 50 000 years?

Most people who get this question will say that we will all be coffee-coloured. I say no. This amount of time will allow for small evolutionary changes. All people living in colder countries, regardless of their origins, will become lighter-skinned to allow the limited sunlight to have maximum effect and the opportunity to absorb sunlight in order to create vitamin D.

All those in very hot countries will become very dark-skinned. Their hair will then thicken and darken to protect themselves from the harshness of the sun. Those in the in-between areas like the Mediterranean will be slightly darker in colour. Of course, this is hypothetical. We are all possibly going to be coffee-coloured if we survive that long because we will all travel, mix in and interbreed. Except for President Trump. He will still be orange.

What does this tell us?

We are all the same beneath the skin. Whether we like it or not. Whatever god you want to prostrate yourself before, we are all the same. Culture, religion etc. are just human constructs that divide us down artificial lines. I think it is sad. I like that there are differences, that we eat different stuff, that we do things slightly differently, that just makes life a little more interesting. We do, however, need to understand that it is entirely due to geographical necessities. We are still all the same underneath the skin.

CCTV

The list of moans and groans about CCTV in police work are many and varied and would fill a not insubstantial tome of tedious invective. So I won't do that. You can have something tedious in an entirely different way.

The police commissioner Condon, who was top johnny banana for the Met for the last seven years of the 90s, once suggested that CCTV would effectively take over policing. He clearly envisaged every square inch of our lives being surveilled by the ubiquitous machines meaning that no one would dare commit a crime for fear that they would be caught in glorious technicolour and brought to justice by officers who sat around offices waiting for a CCTV controller to call them with a name, address and inside leg measurement of the perpetrator. Obviously, a man who thought automatons would take over eventually leaving the commissioner a glorified computer gamer. Didn't happen. Go figure!

We have four basic types of CCTV. Your common-or-garden council-run cameras that are zoomed right back to take an overview of a road or town centre, to be zoomed in whenever an incident is spotted. It doesn't detect faces and registration numbers unless specifically focused by an operator. Then you get your bus and train CCTV which, by its very nature, is zoomed in and picks up close features quite well. It is very good for identifying people. You then get your privately owned CCTV used by shops and private residents. These can be useful on occasions. Then, in London, you get your Transport For London (TFL) cameras. These only record when someone parks their car in the wrong place or drives in a bus lane. Otherwise, it does not record anything unless the police ask them. The operators get very shirty when police ask them to look at things as trivial as rape and murder. 'What about bus lane offenders?' they cry. They could get away with it!

The fact is that I can only remember two occasions when a crime was detected and solved by CCTV, and one of them was directed by police in the first place. The cameras are zoomed out too far to detect facial features, actions or anything useful to an investigation. The only time they were really of any use was when someone was able to give an account of their or someone else's movements that could be tracked using clothing and other obvious identifying features to pick them up.

One of our problems was that the courts would insist on all CCTV to be made available to defence whether it is evidential or supports their defence or not. This flies in the face of what is the legal process and creates a huge, labour intensive burden for virtually no return. Defence lawyers will say things like, "CCTV may assist our defence, we won't know unless we see it." The fact is that all evidence is handed in. It is reviewed by the CPS and police will have an input. The defence gets what is relevant to their defence. If they want something that isn't evidential then they should go out and find it themselves. Stop wasting public finances on the client's whim.

One Sunday morning, I arrived at work to be presented with an incident to investigate. All the information I had to go on was a man in a red car waving a gun around in a small but identifiable area. No evidence of discharge. No descriptions of any people involved. No make, model, size or anything else to do with the car. Just that – man, red car, gun. I went to the area to investigate the incident. I knew it wasn't covered by council CCTV but was in the vicinity of a petrol station. Petrol station equals CCTV, and they are normally looking for registration numbers in case a car drives off without paying. I collected the footage for the appropriate time plus an hour or so either side and went back to the station. I checked the footage taking in the hour either side of the incident in case the video timer was inaccurate. I found that the only thing it had recorded throughout the entire period was the shadow of a person walking close-by out of shot. Not a silhouette, mind you, literally a shadow cast by overhead lights. So I took the videotape (Yes, it was that long ago) and handed it back to the attendant. There was nothing else to investigate. No other sightings, no witnesses, no shots heard, no injuries reported, nothing. So I closed the investigation and forgot about it. A week later on Monday, a colleague approached me. He asked me about the incident. I told him what he already knew. He went on to tell me that a very similar incident had happened over the weekend, but someone had been captured. He said that he would take over my investigation as it was clearly linked and that I need to do nothing further.

Fast forward a year or so. I was called by the officer asking about the CCTV from the incident. I had no memory of the incident at all. It was half an hour of my working life. It was one insubstantial incident among a thousand others over the past year. So I couldn't help. "Well," says the officer, "I'm at court with the case now, and the judge wants to know where the footage is so he could review it. If you can't help, you will have to come to court and tell him." It seems that he had palmed off the blame for this onto me even though he would have been responsible the moment he took over the case. So I returned to the station to apprise myself of the incident. I read my two-line entry and off I went to face the music. I told the judge that I had no real memory, but I had made the entry and that quite clearly stated that there was nothing on the footage. There would be no reason for me to make that entry if it wasn't so. I am told the second incident was pretty self-explanatory as the guy had been caught red-handed. Despite this, the judge dropped both cases and acquitted the defendant because the footage that could help in no way whatsoever was not presented at court. I think that was a case of the judge being a little petulant.

But the system can work. There may be a little give and take but...

The one time that the council did help was as a result of the operators' voyeuristic predilections. Picture the scene. It's a Saturday night. The nightclubs are starting to close up. Plenty of drunk youngsters larking about. Among those youngsters are a goodly proportion of young ladies dressed to impress. One or two, having not being successful in their feminine wiles, are starting to stagger their way home alone. The CCTV operators know that young inebriated females are targeted by the darker elements of our society. So, purely for their own protection (honest guv, trust me, I'm not a policeman), they zoom in on one likely lass. Sometimes, I'm sure as the result of a slip of the hand, the camera got a little too close to certain parts of the lady's anatomy while she wobbled her way along. While this was happening, the young lady was approached by Rodney Robber and his pal who were targeting just this sort of person to rob. So the whole incident was caught on CCTV in close-up. The police, who were close at hand, as the pubs and clubs were kicking out and they always are there at that time, were contacted directly. The CCTV Operators were equipped with police radios so they could speak directly to officers on the scene. They then directed officers to both the victim and the thieves who had no answers to the excellent evidence. Job well done and no mistake!

I should say in fairness that this example of voyeurism is not commonplace. These images are recorded and kept for quite a while. If there was evidence that the operators were just using the system for their own entertainment, it would be picked up by their supervisors and feathers would fly. So they don't... well not often... I don't think.

Occasionally the cameras came in handy for stopping things that were overlooked.

It's the start of night duty. The pubs were kicking out and the streets were full of people going about their business sourcing crap food since they had spent the evening filling their young bodies with crap beer. The weather was clement and there was no angst in the town centre. A colleague and I were taking the opportunity to get out and about and protect the community that we endeavoured to serve.

We spotted something ahead that was something and nothing: a tall, leggy blonde young woman was walking along the pavement at quite a pace. A pace or two behind was a short middle-aged Asian male who appears to be trying to keep up. She steadfastly looked straight ahead as if he didn't exist. There appeared to be nothing to it. It was slightly amusing, but nothing for us to worry about. Five minutes later, in the opposite direction, another tall, leggy young brunette was seen striding down the road. Two paces behind we could see the same short Asian man. Now, this was odd, so we decide to keep an eye on this. We also informed the CCTV operators to do the same. They disappeared from our direct line of sight but 5 minutes later, a different lady, same man. We positioned ourselves at the side of the road so that they would pass close by us to see what if anything was said. We didn't quite hear any conversation but the woman was obviously flustered. So we decided enough is enough. We put ourselves in a position that we could stop the man. We found one of the women involved and spoke to her. She didn't know him but it seemed plain to us that he was trying to get her attention. So we stopped the man knowing that the cameras were on us.

He appeared to be of good character – as in he is not a criminal – but he was hassling women. We could see no laws being broken other than harassment. We considered our options and felt that he should get a flea in his ear and sent on his way – hoping that he would go home.

As we were about to send him on his way. The CCTV operators interjected and suggested that we view their footage. They are 5 minutes away, so he was detained on the street for a little longer under the supervision of some uniformed officers. What we saw, bearing in mind we had the man in our sights for a good 30 minutes was rather embarrassing. All the time he was approaching the women, he had his penis exposed and was trying to get them to look. And neither of us had spotted it.

This was not just flashing, this M&S flashing! This was much more active than just plain, common or garden flashing. He wanted them to stop and take a look.

He was arrested and interviewed by someone else in the morning while I was tucked up safely in my bed. We were told that, under skilful interrogation, he admitted everything adding that he had a very small penis and got his kicks out of nubile young women laughing at his inadequacy. Each to his own.

This next tale-of-woe could come under the interviewing chapter or this. AS the thrust of the example is about how the interviewee reacts to CCTV, it seemed appropriate to put it here.

There are countries out there where the nationals have so little faith in anything to do with authority that they are all taught from when they first learn to talk that if anyone in authority asks them anything, they should lie. It matters not what it is about or why they are asking. If they are in authority, they are the enemy. If they want information, then they want it for a reason, and that reason is not going to be good. So lie about everything.

Ok, this is fine, but in this country, we are taught that honesty is, by and large, the best policy. If we are caught out in a lie, it is a source of extreme embarrassment and should be avoided. People who are taught to lie from an early age, do not have that embarrassment feature in their make-up. At least not when it comes to telling porkies.

I had to deal with a gentleman who had been caught using dodgy credit cards in a large chain store. The investigation had revealed that he favoured this particular chain store and visited several of them buying all a sorts of rubbish because he could afford it... it wasn't his money. All was caught on camera and evidence in the form of receipts and bank accounts had been collected. He was sitting in the interview room complete with a solicitor by his side, pen poised. An interview was started. What follows isn't verbatim. I would never use such closed question techniques. It is just a flavour of what ensued.

Q.   Have you been into TKMaxx in Bromley recently?

A.   No

Q.   Have you bought anything from that shop at any time?

A.   No

Q.   Have you used a credit card in that shop at any time?

A.   No

Q.   Have you used a credit card in the name of Mr (insert name) at any time?

A.   No

Q.   Take a look at the CCTV footage, who is that at the counter?

A.   That is me.

Q.   Do you recognise the shop?

A.   Yes that is TKMaxx.

Q.   Do you know which store it is?

A.   Bromley.

Q.   What are you doing there?

A.   Buying something at the cheque out.

Q.   Here is the till roll, this is the card you used, is it yours?

A.   No.

Q.   Do you know the cardholder?

A.   No.

Q.   Have you been to any other branches anywhere else?

A.   No.

Q.   Have you used a credit card either yours or anyone else's in any TKMaxx

A.   No

Q.   Take a look at this CCTV...

This continued in the same vein for three of four different shops in different towns around South London There was not a single sign of any embarrassment at being caught out, he just kept on going in that vein throughout. I couldn't call him entirely dishonest. He could have said, "No, not me, guv. Must be someone else. Don't know that shop. No, not me, I'm innocent." He just lied, realised that he was rumbled, told the truth then lied when we moved to the next topic.

Speed and other traffic cameras.

I was talking about the Brexit issue with some people when the question was asked, "Why do we need a European parliament when all the member states have their own parliaments, their own fiscal system, their own legislative bodies?" Someone replied, "What about human rights?" Well, here is a thing. The European Commission on Human Rights (ECHR) that got together to discuss this, basically collected all the ideas from all the member states, scrunched it all together and came up with something that was a bridge between those members whose own laws were a little lackadaisical and those who had good a record in this area.

The UK never had a single piece of legislation that dealt specifically with human rights. The individual enactments all had inbuilt sections that tried to ensure the individual rights of people were maintained. Obvious things like the presumption of innocence or innocent until proven guilty. Also one's right to not incriminate oneself – the right to silence. The list is long and not something I will go into, suffice to say that when the ECHR came through with their stuff, the UK didn't have to change anything to remain within their recommendations – and that is all it was, recommendations. The fact is that the stuff we had in place went further than that of the ECHR. We now do have legislation which is in line with much of what they want. It was only since the ECHR that our Human rights started to diminish. We used to have the right to silence. We still do, but there is now a caveat. If you choose not to answer questions in a police investigation, then the jury can draw inference from that silence if you decide to be more co-operative in court. In other words, you can't say nothing in an interview, go home and make up a story with your mates then go to court with this perfectly dove-tailed alibi that all your mates endorse. The judge will just tell the jury to question why you didn't come up with that story when you were first asked and use their discretion to form their final decision. This sort of stuff with the dodgy alibi did use to happen. Don't get me wrong, I agree with this change in the law, but it is a sign that human rights are being diminished to come into line with the EU

Presumption of innocence has also taken a bit of a hit. This is by way of the dreaded ubiquitous traffic camera. If a vehicle bearing your registration number is seen committing a minor road traffic offence like a no right turn, you as the registered keeper are responsible. They do not need to prove whether or not you were driving. They do not care if you were nowhere near your car at the time. Your car, your offence. Pay! Now how is that fair? The last time I received a traffic fine I was actually in Kenya at the time. The fine was issued in Islington, a place with which I am familiar. They didn't care. It used to be that the prosecuting authority had to first prove beyond reasonable doubt that an offence had been committed. Then they had to prove to the same rigid standard who committed it. This duty to prove who committed an offence appears to have all but disappeared for incidents caught on camera. If I was investigating a rape allegation and the registration number of a vehicle came up, the owner would have no obligation to tell me who the driver was. If the person was to say that he wasn't driving it and he doesn't know who was, that would be it. I would have nowhere else to go. I couldn't just assume that person was liable, I would have to prove who was driving at the time. So the result is that I have a traffic offence against me even though I could not possibly have committed it as I was 5000 miles away at the time.

It is slightly different if it is an endorsable offence. But not much. The registered keeper has to give details of the person who was driving. This happened to someone very close to me once. She stated that she was at work at the time of the incident, the car was at home and any one of three other people could have driven it. She had no idea who, and the three weren't going to say. She offered to assist in identifying the driver by viewing the CCTV footage. They sent a picture of the back of the car. No use to man nor beast. They decided that they would prosecute her for failing to provide details of the driver. Fortunately, the court could see that she was trying to assist and acquitted her. My problem was that they felt they had no obligation to properly investigate. An offence was committed, someone has to pay and we have decided it's your turn. This isn't human rights, there should be a presumption of innocence and a requirement for the authorities to present a cogent case to the courts. Would it be acceptable for her to just give details of someone who she thought was driving regardless of evidence or lack thereof? I think not. I couldn't send someone to court just because I had found his DNA near a crime scene. I had to investigate it. So should they.

On another occasion, I received a fine through the post for failing to give way at a give way sign. I knew I was driving on this occasion but knew I hadn't failed to give way at any point during the journey. To prove a breach of a give way sign, the prosecutors have to prove that I crossed the broken white lines of the Give Way sign and, as a direct result of my actions, another vehicle was forced to alter speed or direction. So I checked the footage. There I was crossing the broken white lines. As I passed over them, another car came into view going very slowly. I cleared the intersection before the other vehicle was anywhere near. At no time did it slow down, speed up or change direction for any reason, much less my actions. Clearly, no offence was committed. So I went onto the website to tell them I was not guilty. There was nothing on there that allowed me to deny the allegation on the basis that 'it never happened'. You either pay up or tell them that your car was stolen or sold prior to the offence. So I had to resort to writing a letter explaining the facts and informing them that, as no offences were committed, I would not be paying and that they would have to take me to court if they disagreed. They gave in. This shows that they believe that they need to do nothing other than to identify an offence and send a fine out. Most people would have paid up on that one so they are getting away with it.

It is stated in law that councils cannot use traffic cameras as a means of income. They can only target an area if there has been a specific traffic problem that needed to be resolved. Like for example, A stretch of road where some fatalities have occurred due to speeding cars. Councils ignore this out of hand. There are two speed cameras on my road. I have lived here for nearly 30 years and in that time, there have been two fatal accidents, neither being as a result of speed. The area that I got the 'give way' fine was a short section of road that narrows to one lane due to a bridge. There is a give way sign allowing priority to cars in one direction so that no one gets stuck halfway through. I have never had an issue at this bridge. The system works pretty well – no snarl-ups, no angst, no crashes. So the camera is there purely for getting money into the coffers. I have to say that I would much prefer to be stopped by a patrolling officer and directly accused of committing some traffic indiscretion. At least he would be there to assess the circumstances and make a reasonable decision based on his knowledge and experience.

I recall a well-publicised case when a government minister got caught out. The story was that he got his wife to take the points for a speeding offence that he had committed. Of course, the couple had a falling out a few years later. Such was the acrimony between the two, she told the world that this had happened. There was all sorts of finger-wagging and breast-beating and tut-tutting about people in authority being dishonest. Lots of heads rolled and everyone lost. My point was totally different from everyone else's. While everyone was getting all political about it, they seemed to forget that if the prosecutors didn't know who was driving the vehicle, they had no business issuing the fine and endorsing the license in the first place. Surely the prosecution has to have a case before they can start issuing fines. I am fully aware that people in positions of responsibility should be more honest, but politicians just aren't that. Of course, if they get caught out, then they take the consequences which should be swift and firm. Wouldn't it be so nice to see politicians getting punished for dishonesty? It would feel like you are punishing a banker for lending money and charging interest. This doesn't even deal with the issue that we do not have to say anything that would incriminate ourselves. I think this is government – and it is not party-political, this goes across the board – taking the easy option instead of the correct one. Yes, there may be more court cases but if the investigators are getting it right, then that should mitigate any real problems.

As a final swing at this area of investigation, I will look at a case that I dealt with involving recorded footage. It wasn't CCTV, but it had the same effect and shows that there are things that video footage will never pick up on. This involved a pub licensee and a punter. The police received a call after a woman banged on a door neighbouring the pub she ran. She was in a high emotional state, her clothes torn and dishevelled and her hair and make-up ruined. She took some time to calm down but managed to get the message across that she had been raped. We arrived and started the investigation. A suspect was soon identified and arrested. Mobile phones were seized as was necessary in most cases and they were sent off to the lab for forensic downloading. The suspect was interviewed in which he stated that it was all consensual. She approached him just as the final punters were leaving and suggested that he stay behind. He told us that the conversation was all recorded on her phone. She wanted to record their 'liaison' and struggled a little to work out how to operate the device. He was adamant that the examination of her phone would reveal all. She was interviewed and gave a consistent account of a very violent encounter. We walked away from the initial part of the investigation feeling convinced that she was the genuine victim of a violent attack in the pub after the doors were closed. The way she presented to the neighbour, what she said, how she said it, her state of dress all pointed to this being the case.

We followed protocol and continued the investigation to ensure all avenues were explored. Unfortunately, when we viewed the footage from her phone, it became apparent that she was very much the mover-and-shaker. She made all the moves. She used unambiguous language to tell him exactly what she required of him. He was the willing follower. The footage ended before anything sexual actually happened, but we were left in no doubt that she had lied to us. We had never been so convinced by an allegation before – no-one other than an accomplished actor could have pulled off that performance if it was all a lie. We had no choice but to speak to the victim and confront her with this pretty damning evidence. She was devastated at the evidence but insisted that she was raped.

I spent some time trying to work out what happened here. The only thing I could come up with was that, once the phone had been turned off, he became violent. She was obviously willing to have sex but was not willing to put up with violence. As soon as that started, she withdrew consent, as is her absolute right, but he continued. The whole thing scared her very badly. Despite this, she decided to brush over the fact that she made all the moves at the start. Unfortunately, this woman had been raped that evening but because she wasn't honest from the start – and I have covered what happens at court when a victim is found to be dishonest - he got away with it. Consent can be withdrawn at any point. Anything that happens beyond that point is done without consent. Juries will often take a dim view of consent being randomly withdrawn, but if there are valid reasons, as there were in this case, then there shouldn't be a problem. So video footage is helpful but often poses as many questions as it answers

Media

Love them or hate them, they are here with us. Freedom of the press overrides everything. It matters not if, in printing their story, an entire population is wiped out. People have a right to know. The media have this awful habit of getting people worked up about things that are happening all around us every day without our knowing anything about the issues involved. If they get a bee in their bonnet about something, they gather a load of stats, publish them over a few weeks drawing all kinds of newspaper-selling inferences. The public start panicking as they think that there is a new crime epidemic out there. In fact, in most cases, little has changed other than the fact that the public now actually know that the 'something' that was happening can be quantified. All carefully edited so we don't know any more than what they think we ought to know. Rodney Robber is going to be out there nicking mobile phones off young kids. Johnny Joyrider, likewise, is going to be 'borrowing' other people's cars whether or not we know it is happening. If we were made aware of half of the stuff going on out there, we would never leave our front door. Not that it is complete mayhem out there, it isn't. But publishing numbers and suggesting the problem can be worse than the actual issues. It sells newsprint and that it all that matters.

That being said, 90% of media articles in this day and age are the opinion of the editors. I do not give a toss what the editor of any news outlet does or does not think. I want to know the facts and an unbiased background. This does not happen anymore. The BBC carried out a rather unscientific herd-mentality test once. What happened was that ten people were stood in a line and asked a series of simple questions. The first nine were all stooges, the last in line was the unsuspecting guinea pig and had no idea what the experiment was all about. Questions were asked, and each had to answer in turn, in the presence and hearing of all the others. One question that they asked was very simple. One that everyone knew. The first nine were instructed to give the same incorrect answer to see what the last person would do. So, the question was something like, 'what is the capital of France?' The answer to be given by all 9 was 'Madrid'. The woman at the end was clearly confused and extremely hesitant but, in the end, answered 'Madrid'. Herd mentality in action.

So what do we learn from this? The majority of us would be saying, "Well, I wouldn't fall for that." I suppose the unfortunate woman would have said the same. So we learn nothing. What the BBC learned was that it works really well. All they have to say is 'most people believe...' and they know that people at home would be thinking, "Well if everyone thinks it, then it must be true therefore that is what I think." The BBC is one of the worst exponents of the side of the media that are of the opinion that everyone should think what the BBC believe we should think. Whenever I hear this – and it does happen often enough – I close down and treat the information with the utmost suspicion.

How many times have we seen a story where the media picks up on something, manages to find out who the bad guy is and proceed to do a hatchet job on the person? Trial by media is what the media itself has dubbed it. If the bad guy isn't hung, drawn and quartered within 5 minutes of the article's publication, the police are vilified. If the person is dealt with and ultimately found to be innocent, the media seem to go very quiet. If the person is found guilty then subsequently found to have been incorrectly convicted, the media will completely forget what their coverage was all about and round on the police for harassing innocent members of the public. There are plenty of examples. Because the media does not have to be 'forensic' in their investigations, they can say what they like, put it down to a protected informant and walk away from their obligations. The legal process has not had that advantage. Police cannot comment on things if they are 'sub judices' nor can those involved in civil proceedings for the same reason. The press, however, seems to think it is perfectly OK to ask a question to which the answer is subject to these laws, then deliberately draw incorrect inferences from the ensuing silence. This happens daily.

Let us take the press coverage of the anti-Semitic debate in the Labour Party. I am not party political in any way. I do not believe something on the basis that one party or the other says so. I will not base my opinion on the colour of tie some politician chooses to wear. I want to hear evidence and then make my own mind up. I will say that I do not believe that the Labour leader, Mr Corbyn is now, nor was ever anti-Semitic. Certain sections of the media, while not directly accusing him personally, have sought to implicate him in anti-Israeli sentiments within the party. I don't think he liked how the Israeli government dealt with the Palestinian issue, but that doesn't mean he has a problem with the Jewish community, just Israeli politics. They are separate issues. His faults are many and varied as are his good points. This, in my view, was a campaign by right-wing activists trying – and in my opinion, succeeding – to draw attention away from his methods and his politics. It is fashionable within the media to repeat a question until they get an answer that they want. Politicians have a habit of not answering questions. If they do, they will always try to bring the subject matter onto what they want to talk about. This has happened since the dawn of time. We are all aware of the Michael Howard interview where he was asked a pertinent question and steadfastly avoided answering the question. The interviewer just carried on asking the same question over and over. This was fine and, at the time, it was about time someone did it. Over the ensuing years, other interviewers have tried the same tactic. But what they often do, is ask questions that the interviewee can clearly never give an accurate answer, then keep going. In doing so, they draw – or at least invite the audience to draw – the incorrect conclusion that the politician is avoiding a question.

So, in 2019 a political pundit on the BBC tried this tactic with Mr Corbyn. He was asked if he was going to apologise to the Jewish community for his party's stand on anti-Semitism. It was an impossible question to answer. I believe it was asked because it was impossible to answer and I believe the interviewer was, at best, being disingenuous. Although he didn't hold those views and did not believe that his party as a whole did either, he couldn't just say he wasn't going to apologise, as the response by the media would have been to tell the world that he was a holocaust denier and that he was not going to deal with an insidious problem within his party. Nor could he respond by apologising to the Jewish community because he would be doing so for something he and his party did not do or think. So he was between a rock and a hard place. All he could do was to say that cases of prejudice would be dealt with as appropriate when the incidents were brought to his attention. The interviewer knew that Corbyn could never give a satisfactory answer. Knowing this, he just kept asking it. It was like the guy was directly accusing him of being an anti-Semite without having to say it out loud. I believe he – the interviewer – was a coward and should have been outed at the time.

This was followed by a half-hearted attempt to show the Tory party to be Islamophobic. It fell on deaf ears because, although there may well be Islamophobes in the party in the same way as there may be anti-Semites in the Labour party, it could not accurately be ascribed to the party as a whole.

We then have the thorny issue of terrorism. England has been subject to politicised violence for decades. The reasons vary depending on one's political viewpoint. When the IRA were out and about, they wanted to get their message across, but to do that they needed to be funded. They got most of this from the USA. The population of the USA were always a little squeamish about women and children dying. This meant that the IRA attacked financial targets and avoided 'collateral damage' as far as they could. The Islamic fundamentalists who seem to have taken over from the IRA, do not appear to be bothered about the loss of life. Indeed some, it would seem, aim at maximising it. What they both do have in common is the 'oxygen of publicity'. They need this to encourage their supporters to finance their campaigns. The Media provide this and more. One weapon we can use against terrorism is to starve them of publicity, The media, however, are too concerned about selling copy. They will run any story about a death that may involve terrorism to distraction. They will analyse, dissect and pontificate. None of the information we are getting, beyond the basic facts, is really new to us, it is just rehashed and carted out every time a new incident happens. By doing this, the organisations who seek to blow us all to hell in a hand-basket are getting free prime-time publicity. The sort that cost most of us thousands of pounds a minute. I question why we need this coverage. If a terrorist incident happens, an article telling us the basic details with little or no mention of terrorists and no speculation whatsoever would suffice. Thereafter, the media should simply cut them off. In this way, we the general public, are informed of what is happening and don't have to put up with the dodgy subjective reporting of the news media. Our tormentors then get nothing other than the fact that they have caused a little disruption. Please note that I do not single out any particular news outlet nor do I comment on the type of media. This is because they are all at it and are all as bad as each other.

Clearly, the media can help in the investigation of crime, but they have to be distanced from the investigation. This is because any trial that involves an incident that the media has had an interest in, has the possibility of influencing the jury – something I am sure they would love to do.

In the first few years of my career, I became aware of a man who had been caught on camera holding a bank up at gunpoint. A colleague of mine had recognised him on a TV appeal and phoned it in. The man was arrested, charged, went to trial and convicted. I knew this person as he was a person of interest in the area that I patrolled regularly. I was pootling around on one of my patrols one day and came across him wandering around as free as a bird a year after the incident. We had a chat, something that I did regularly with these sort of people as I felt I needed to know my 'enemy'. He told me that his legal team appealed the conviction because the photograph used in the TV appeal was the same as the one used in the trial. This, according to the judge, adversely affected the decision of the jury. They won the appeal and he was released. There was no doubt that he knew that he had got away with it and would rightly have spent a long time in prison. He had no qualms about admitting that it was him in the picture.

The investigator and the media should have had knowledge of what they could and could not do. The police took the blame – probably rightly – but the media didn't. They know what they can and can't do and they know that if they breach the rules, they won't suffer. They never even acknowledged fault.

Now here is a thing. Circa 2011 the media got into a spot of bother surrounding bribing police for information. We aren't talking about chucking trials or 'relocating' drug hauls. It was more about getting the inside lines on stories before their rivals. It came off the back of a situation that the government tasked police to investigate It was a media-led issue surrounding politicians claiming expenses for very dodgy reasons. The police, to the absolute horror of the politicians who ordered the investigation, started actually investigating. What was supposed to happen is that the police would push a few paper clips around a desk for a month or two, ask a few very tame, prepared questions of a select few cabinet ministers then let it all slide. The politicians could then claim to have been investigated and found to be in the clear. The police can say they did their investigation and they would be backed up.

What actually happened is that they investigated properly and found that there was a bucket load of politicians taking liberties. It was endemic across the political spectrum. The politicians then got very hot under the collar and set the media onto the police. Allegations that the media always appeared to be ahead of the curve abounded. The only way this could have happened was if they had inside information. No one believed that information like that would be free.

So heads rolled. Some of the more lurid and sensational rags died. Some media moguls answered a few awkward questions. Those media outlets who weren't caught in the field of fire all tut-tutted away at the nasty gutter press while breathing heavy sighs of relief that they weren't caught out themselves. And make no mistake, they were all at it… with the possible exception of Private Eye and one or two others. Interestingly, in the subsequent enquiry, they decided that the police were entirely at fault. The press, on the other hand, were not. This is not reasonable. Apparently, if there are no people to corrupt, the corrupters won't have anyone to corrupt. Yeah, Right!

This is interesting because the law moguls believe that, in the world of drug abuse, the dealers – i.e. the corrupters – are the main villains and the drug users – the corrupted – are effectively the victims. Pretty much opposite to corruption. In both cases, you can't have the one without the other but specifically in the case of the press. There are few if any cases where the police have gone looking to media outlets for bribes. The press have always initiated, so I think this decision was a very political one. Let's face it the politicians need the press more than the police. Especially if the police aren't playing ball! I may be considered somewhat cynical if I were to suggest that the drug dealers don't pay taxes on their ill-gotten gains. Just like those taking the bribes. Whereas the drug user and the corrupter are laying money out so don't come into the taxman's purview. No, far too cynical, that can't be right!

I would like to think that most editors and journalists are decent upstanding members of the community. What that means that it is purely circulation issues and how well their news stories sell that dictates the timbre of the stories. It is sad that newspapers primarily, but also other media outlets feel that only bad news sells. To me, it beggars belief that these institutions should want to diminish the efficacy of the police. They will say they are holding the police to account. I agree that this is absolutely required. But to the point of lying – at least by omission – I think is a step too far.

I saw two social media posts today. One saying, "Hate Police? The next time you need help, call a crackhead." A bit brutal but there is a message there. I might also suggest that going to your local social services wouldn't be that much help unless you wanted to just talk about it, hold meetings about it, pontificate ad nauseum about the woes of the world but actually do nothing. Your local solicitor wouldn't be interested either unless you had money to pay for his time, and even then, he would just feign interest. In fact, only police, ambulance/NHS and the fire services are going to be of any use because they are the doers of our society. The other post said, "To those who hate the police, please be aware, we also hate you, but if you are in trouble, we will come to your rescue even at the risk to our own safety." I'm not sure that I 'hated' everyone who wasn't police. In fact, I know that. Most of my friends were not police officers. Some were even suspicious of the organisation. But again, there is a message there that the media doesn't like to make plain – the police will put their own safety on the line for the sake of total strangers.

Another social media post that was going around several years ago caught my attention as I thought there was a ring of truth to it. It was an American guy walking along the road speaking into a video recorder on a selfie stick. He was explaining that he had spent his entire life breaking the law and paying the consequences for it. He wasn't boasting, he was just being factual. He stated that in all his years as an active criminal, he was never abused, physically or verbally by any member of their law enforcement services. This, he said, was because he was always compliant. He knew that if he fought, they would fight back, and he would lose. So he didn't. As a result, he was never attacked verbally or physically. His message was to the other criminals out there. He was telling them that if they didn't want to be attacked, just comply. His message was, "it isn't police brutality, it's resisting arrest." If you don't resist, no brutality will come your way. I am sure that there are police out there who are gratuitously violent. I never came across any myself but, they represent our community and, like it or like it not, there are elements of our community that are gratuitously violent. We try to weed them out but some will always slip through the net. So this man was saying that he knew that he was being detained because he was a criminal. But he also said that if he was innocent – which wasn't often – then in general, that would become apparent. The police were not his enemy, just a consequence of his chosen lifestyle.

Throughout my entire thirty years, I was forced to use violence twice. I didn't avoid confrontation in general. In fact, I was always quite busy. I just found ways of calming situations or finding someone who could. If someone didn't want to calm down – i.e. they were spoiling for a fight – I was not the man you were going persuade into violence. So all those members of the public who we see on our television screens being beaten up by police conveniently caught on someone's mobile, just consider what happened immediately prior to the footage. The bit that equally conveniently did not reach the media. I saw a picture in the papers just a week ago. It was a photo of a London police officer punching a demonstrator. It looked awful. Then someone of the social media set helpfully found the footage and put up the frames that immediately preceded the punch. This showed footage of the apparent victim throwing a punch and connecting with the officer and the officer reacting in self-defence. The film was obviously sequential, and the first bit was obviously deliberately removed by the media to tell a story. Not one of an officer defending himself as was obvious but one of police brutality.

I also found that if I was demonstrably calm and non-confrontational while, at the same time, not backing away, the general public would be supportive regardless of the situation. I have, on more than one occasion, been in a situation where I was on my own without means of communication with my colleagues and in a situation that offered no retreat. On one occasion, this was on public transport. I was returning home after a long day at work. I was approached by a very aggressive black youth who I had interrupted while he was graffitiing up a tram stop. I had simply wiped off the graffiti before it has a chance to dry thereby destroying his 'tag'. He took offence to this and after we had got onto the tram, he stood nose to nose with me shouting, swearing and trying to get me to strike out first. His posse was hanging around further down the carriage and I realised it would have been carnage if the situation deteriorated. I stood my ground, said nothing at all and maintained eye contact. When he finally realised that I wasn't going to react and possibly realising that the general mood of the passengers on the tram was turning against him, he withdrew to where his mates were. One of the other passengers – another black youth – told me that he and his mates were ready and willing to come to my aid. They felt that I should have just decked the idiot. I wanted to myself, but he would have won if I had and I wasn't going to be beaten by a half-wit scrote-bag like that. I thanked the guys for their support. As an experiment, I stepped off the tram at a stop prior to the one I wanted. The gang also stepped off so I stepped back on again. They followed suit and stepped back on. The train scene in the film 'The French Connection' appeared to be being played out here. When I got to my stop and they got out so I stayed on and got out at the next stop. this was just a slightly longer walk through a park but safer for it. There were police everywhere when I walked through the park. It had become apparent that the rest of the passengers had also come to my rescue and had called the cavalry. I had already cued up my wife to get the car as close to the tram stop as possible (About 400 yards). I went straight into the car and left the scene unscathed.

It is something that the media would deny vociferously, but it is my contention that the media are the most powerful organisation in this and many other countries. They go throughout the world reporting on issues in all other countries. Issues that we have no idea about. They also obviously report on events in this country, but they will know that only a handful of people will know the truth of each incident, so they can just twist it to make their own story, knowing that a few peoples' voices are never going to penetrate the wall that is the media. It seems that they are willing to take an event and provide a headline that will put their slant on whatever has happened. They then write a paragraph describing the issue in brief, then spend the rest of the column expounding on what their opinions are. As we have no idea of what is happening on the ground, they can pretty much say what they like. I spent a lot of time in Africa and saw at first-hand what they did to create headlines. Throwing a load of sweets at a dustbin and filming the children apparently having to scavenge for food. Filming a few African men enjoying the sun in one of the local parks. Sounds ok? If you take the photograph from behind some railings, in a manner that makes it look like they have been left to die in an enclosure, a different story emerges. This all sounds a bit twee, but they are forming opinions in people who think they know what is happening abroad. I have already mentioned the herd mentality thing. It is happening all around. I read newspapers, I read the headline, I then read the first paragraph then move on to the next story. I have no interest in what the editor of the Times thinks about anything at all. I just want facts. I will make up my own mind what the underlying issues are.

I have had several discussions with an acquaintance that I met in Greenwich Market in London. He is firmly left of any political spectrum you care to use. He only reads the Guardian, does not watch any TV and is only interested in what the Labour Party has to say politically. He believes he has a world view on all his opinions but without knowing what other people, papers, or any other type of outlet says, how can he know anything other than what the Guardian and the Labour Party want him to think? I prefer to get my information from as many sources as possible and make my own decisions. Unfortunately, I don't know all the facts because my only source of any information outside my own personal circle is through the media and they don't always deal in facts. I therefore have a problem knowing what is fact and what is fiction. I muddle through, but I have trust issues where the media is concerned

Take, for example, the issue with youths going around stabbing each other. From a global perspective, the violence issues that we experience in the UK are minuscule when compared with many other countries around the world. This, of course, does not mean we don't need to be concerned, we just need perspective. The media have decided that we need to know about these stabbings so they publish figures every time a young boy dies. This means that we all know that young boys are dying. We knew this before, but it was never quantified. Now that it is, people think that we have a problem that is spiralling out of control. The politicians, keen to get their dishonest faces on the telly, jump on the bandwagon and wag their fingers and tell everyone what a priority it is and that too many young people are dying. Then everyone thinks, well if the politicians are all over it, it must be a problem. It is a problem. But it isn't that big and when the media get bored with this story and stop reporting it – and they will – it will carry on, we just won't hear about it. We will know that it continues but it won't be an issue. What will be a big issue is whatever the media decide is a big issue. Breast beating will then start on that subject.

I heard an interesting statistic today from Mr Alfie Moore, an ex-cop, comedian and podcast meister extraordinaire. He stated that there were 3000 complaints of police violence in England and Wales in the last year. This seems a lot of violence within one organisation. But then take into account how many police officers there are out there – 30 000 in the met alone – and then compare that with the – and I'm quoting directly here – 23 394 assaults on police in the same period in the same area. One every 22 minutes.

If the Media were to be all over the first figure and, if they were of a mind, they could start highlighting stories every time a complaint is made. There would be several stories every day in the papers. Just shy of nine a day throughout the country. People would then start believing that one of the least violent police services in the world has a problem with violence. Imagine if they were to highlight every time a police officer was assaulted. There wouldn't be enough air time on TV or column inches in the newspapers.

Myth Buster

It is a sad fact that much of the fiction that people view on TV in the form of crime dramas and such like are transformed into fact in many of their minds. This idea that a lawyer would march into the custody suite and demand that their client is either charged or released is nonsense. Their role is to advise their client. If they find what they feel is a breach of their client's rights, they will obviously raise the issue but, this is rare indeed. Everything is recorded in this day and age. Every police action is open to scrutiny. The police officers know this and so do not play fast and loose with detainee's rights.

Another myth is this thing about the power of arrest. I had a TV programme on in the background the other day. It was a drama about a unit within the Met that took on retired police officers as civilian investigators. This is not an unusual practice in real life although they tend to act as a support to the police investigators. At one point in the show, one of the old boys makes an arrest. Their reason was that their prime suspect was threatening to slip away. All hell then breaks loose when the solicitor finds out that the arresting officer was a civilian with no powers of arrest. Therefore his actions were unlawful and any evidence obtained thereafter was inadmissible in court. In real life, he would be neglecting his duty if he did *not* detain the suspect. The fact is that the powers that members of the public have to detain people are not that different from the police. The Police and Criminal Evidence Act 1984 (PACE) gives police power to arrest people if they have reasonable grounds to believe an offence either has been, is being, or is about to be committed and they have reasonable grounds to believe that the individual they have in mind is, or is about to be responsible for that offence. The general public is allowed to detain someone if they have reasonable grounds to believe that an offence has been, or is being committed and that the person is likewise responsible. They are hardly going to take powers away from civilian investigators or PCSOs... although PCSOs are actively discouraged from doing anything like this. So they have the same powers as the general public. Having said all that, I have never seen a police officer arresting someone who was about to commit an offence. Although the power is there, it is pretty useless as, without evidence of an actual offence, there is nothing much they can do with it. (We have to bear in mind that an attempt to commit an offence is an offence in itself, so, in that case, they are not about to do anything, they are in the act of attempting). Therefore we can see that in practice, the police powers are almost exactly the same as that of the general public.

Something that TV dramas like to portray is the interdepartmental rivalries. It is true that some departments, like the murder investigation teams, seem to feel that they are superior to everyone else. This is really nothing more than banter. Most departments stick to their own areas of expertise but maintain strong inter-departmental co-operation. The idea that some copper would start complaining when he makes an arrest then sees some other department take over is just never going to happen. Most would be glad to see the whole thing taken on by someone else. Less work for themselves. It doesn't happen much because everyone is busy with their own stuff. The last thing they need is more work and taking on an unsolved crime is just potentially diminishing their own stats. It does happen the other way around, though. Where someone would go into the robbery squad office, for example, and tell them that they have a robbery to investigate. "No," says the DI, "that isn't a robbery, that's 'theft with violence'. Entirely different, go away and sort it out yourself". So the officer slinks away, investigates it fully, then, just as he is about to charge the suspect with robbery, the DI descends and takes over the investigation now that all the leg work has been done. He would then strut about telling everyone that the investigation was poorly handled and their department would have done a much better job. Much mutterings from the person who actually did the leg work with under-the-breath suggestions about where he could shove his investigation, then carry on as usual.

A few other quick ones. How many cop dramas suggest that the accused person is in trouble because they can't prove their innocence? They don't have to, the police have to prove their guilt. If a police officer arrests but does not caution a suspect, that would, at worst render the arrest unlawful and, at best, render all verbal evidence obtained inadmissible. But who would know? The officer is hardly going to waltz into the custody suite ad say, "morning sarge, I've just nicked this guy and ignored all the provisions of PACE. Is that ok?" So these dramas that show people being released because of some procedural indiscretion is a fiction. Either the indiscretion did not happen or the officer is not going to admit it. CSI [insert town] is a fiction. Nothing in these programmes bare any relation to real life. I started watching one once. I couldn't get through a whole episode after a scene where the scientists tell everyone that they have extracted fibre from the body of the murder victim. It is evidently from a red woollen jersey. Therefore it stood to reason in their minds that the murderer must have been wearing a red woollen jersey... "oh, look, there is a bloke wearing a red woollen jersey over there. That must be your man. Case closed, next case please!" Would that it were that easy. There would never be a possibility that someone else who had a red jumper had been in contact but had nothing to do with the offence. Even someone walking past could theoretically pass on a single fibre. Search warrants are not required in many circumstances. There are all manner of things written into legislation that relegate search warrants to the second league. Officers can't just breeze into your house whenever it takes their fancy, there are plenty of rules, but warrants are relatively unusual.

Traffic

Most police don't like dealing with traffic issues. This is mainly because normal, everyday, otherwise law abiding people get caught in its web. Most police officers want to deal with nasty people and take them off the streets. They do not want to antagonise otherwise decent people. It goes without saying that it's a job that needs to be done as people die on our streets due to bad driving. But who hasn't gone over the speed limit? How many of us hasn't come to a complete stop at a stop sign? Who hasn't taken an amber light when they could have stopped safely? Not many. 95% of people will admit to doing it at least occasionally, Of the other 5%, most of them are lying.

I've driven motor cars since 1977 when I was 16 (it was Africa, you can get a car license at 16). I have driven in cities and in the country. In all that time, I have been involved in one incident when I was a learner driver and a recent incident that was entirely my fault. Other than that, I have been involved in no major traffic incidents. I wouldn't say I'm a great driver. Having a police driving course is always going to help, but I have never been particularly interested in the mechanics of driving. I have also cycled around London and the country for many years. I was only ever a commuter cyclist other than a Lands End to John O'Groats challenge that I completed in 9 days over a distance of a little less than 1000 miles (1600 Km) that nearly killed me. So I am not one of those angry club cyclists that think that everyone should get out of their way. Nor am I the guy who wobbles around uncertainly and gives drivers heart attacks. It is the quickest way to get around London bar none. I make sure that if there is anything silly going on, it happens away from me. I am vulnerable as a cyclist and if I keep telling myself that, I stay out of trouble

It is my abiding opinion that cyclists are their own worst enemy. They wind up motorists by cycling in the middle of the road and not allowing them to get past. I'm sure if these same people were in a car with another motorist ahead of them going at 10 miles an hour, they would get the hump. They are so selfish and then wonder why motorists get angry with them.

I personally don't cross traffic lights at red when I am cycling. I think they could change the law to allow this on some T junctions where a cyclist wouldn't impede any other vehicles, but until they do that, I won't. The reason why I don't do this isn't because it's illegal. Not doing something because it is illegal is a rubbish reason. Most people won't nick an unoccupied car if they walked past it. And the reason isn't because it is illegal, its because they believe that it isn't a nice thing to do. So I don't ignore traffic lights for two other reasons: the first is that I am almost 60 and I get tired. A little rest at a traffic light is always welcome. I sometimes get the hump when the light stays on green as I approach them. Second is that motorists get wound up by cyclists breaking rules that the motorists would get done for. Motor cars are bigger than me and I don't want to get into arguments with them, I would probably lose. Its thirty seconds out of my life. It isn't going to hurt.

I can also tell you that I do not undertake lorries unless I have no other choice. I saw a head-cam video of a cyclist once. People publish these pieces of footage to show how bad drivers are. This was the reason for this post, but it only showed how stupid the cyclist ahead of him was and how doubly stupid he, the camera wielding cyclist was for following him. The footage showed a cyclist going up the inside of a stationary HGV waiting at a red traffic light indicating to turn left. The cyclist ahead of the camera, rode straight along the inside and stopped immediately in front of the vehicle's wing mirror, giving the driver absolutely no chance of seeing him. The person with the camcorder followed the idiot and stopped a little way behind along the nearside of the lorry. The lorry then pulled away when the lights turned and whacked the cyclist over the head with the wing mirror. The cyclist fell off his bicycle and had to be treated for serious injuries to his wounded pride. There was no evidence that it knocked any sense into him. The lorry driver remained oblivious to the fact he had struck the man. They would therefore not have known that in knocking the guy off his bicycle, they quite possibly saved his life. Had he stayed on the road, he would have been crushed as the lorry made it's left turn. These are the people who are getting killed on our streets. Undertaking left turning lorries is suicidal. It isn't the lorry driver's fault when he injures cyclists who don't understand this. I don't know how many lorry drivers have been prosecuted after killing a cyclist in this fashion. I imagine that it is a low number as the cyclist is often the one at fault.

Although I know several people who dealt with the investigation of fatal accidents. I have no actual figures of the number of deaths involving cyclists and the causal factors, but my belief, based on experience, is that very few if any cyclists get knocked over while going through a red traffic lights. They aren't stupid, they know that they're vulnerable, they don't do it when there are cars approaching the junction. The only real accidents are caused by vehicles coming out of side streets and not looking properly and cyclists undertaking cars and lorries while they're stationary or in very slow moving traffic. So don't do it. Overtaking is so much safer, oncoming car drivers can see you, the stationary car drivers can see you better in their driver's wing mirror. The blind spot on the drivers side is much smaller, and you can always slip into the stationary line of traffic if there are cars coming. The passenger of a car will often want to get out, giving little or no warning. The door is then opened in front of you giving you no time to react. This rarely happens on the driver's side We drive on the left in this country. Many drivers don't bother to indicate left but they almost always do so when intending to turn right. This means that when a cyclist is approaching stationary cars, they don't know the intentions of the driver when there is no indication. However, they will normally know if the car is indicating to turn right. So it is safer all around to approach and pass the vehicle on the driver's side. You could sit in the traffic jam if you want, I've seen it happen, but that seems to fly in the face of the whole reason for cycling.

On a side note, our relationship with motor vehicles is strange. If a car is involved all the rules seem to change. If your house is burgled and £1500 worth of stuff is stolen. The burglar would probably receive a substantial custodial sentence. If Johnny Joyrider nicks a £50 000 car, it will be more like a slap on the wrist and don't do it again! If someone waves around a weapon in a very irresponsible manner and someone accidentally dies as a result, this could be manslaughter. The offender would receive a substantial custodial sentence. If Johnny Joyrider nicks a car and accidentally runs over a kills someone while he is pratting about with it, this is death by dangerous driving. Judges tend to hand down relatively small custodial sentences for this. If someone buys a guitar for £3000, I'd expect him to take care and go to all sorts of lengths to keep it safe from damage or theft. Buy a £50 000 car and it gets left out in the rain at the side of the road ready for Johnny Joyrider to nick or some idiot to key it because he is jealous. And it may get cleaned once a month. No one considers anyone who speeds in a car a criminal despite the fact that the person is actually breaking the law and risking other peoples' lives. Any other offence where you were endangering people's lives while breaking the law would land you in prison.

Speeding is a £60 fine and points on your license, often followed by a hike in insurance premiums.

Yellow Lines

When I was a young copper on the beat, the police were responsible for enforcing parking regulations. They did this in the form of the much reviled traffic wardens. As reviled as they were, at least they weren't there to help swell the local authority's coffers. Their job was to keep traffic flowing. How well or not they did is a matter of personal opinion and debate, but that was why they were out and about. You wouldn't find them out on the streets 10 minutes before the restrictions ended to try to catch people nicking the last 5 minutes and ticketing them. The local authorities take great pleasure in doing this. It is their best time to be out issuing tickets. Never mind that the cars are causing no traffic issues at 6.25 in the evening.

There was some misunderstanding of the rules. Some people seemed to think parking on a double yellow was much worse than a single. In fact it has no effect on the severity, only the times the restrictions were in force. A single yellow line meant that the local authorities could restrict street parking between 7am to 7pm at least four days and up to seven days a week. Any less than that, they would have to lay broken yellow lines and anything over that, double yellow lines. So if they wanted restrictions to last until 9pm, double yellows it was. You could still stop there to load or unload for 5 minutes unless there were curb markings restricting this.

It was the interpretation that always got me. A traffic warden would see a car on a yellow line. Cars can stop in these areas briefly for the purposes of loading and unloading and normally five minutes was given. Traffic wardens made a decision that only vans could stop in these areas because cars were not big enough to hold anything heavy enough. They would therefore issue a ticket immediately without waiting to see if it was loading or unloading. Tell that to an electrician with a tool box that weighed 50kg. What are we saying here? That they have to lug that beast around with them by foot? I think not. For all that, I think at least it is better than what we have now. Local authority traffic wardens would deliberately avoid busy areas to avoid confrontation. This is stupid. It is the busy areas that need the attention because that is where bad parking causes problems. Oh, I forgot, they aren't there to deal with traffic problems. They are there to issue tickets to provide an income for the local authorities.

And another thing! The timing rules for yellow lines changed without so much as a whisper from anyone. I went into Croydon one evening and found a single yellow line. It was 7.30pm, I knew I was OK so I parked up properly. I wasn't even aware that the local authorities had taken over the parking enforcement. When I returned an hour later, there was a ticket. Apparently, the Local Authorities can make up the rules as they go along now. Yellow lines just mean that there are parking restrictions. It is for the driver to find out what they are from area to area. The Council authorities are only required to put up a sign at the entrance to a parking zone, but that zone could cover a vast area. You just don't know what they are or where the restrictions start of finish unless you are looking out for the signs. These will often be a mile away from where you are stopping. On this occasion, the council decided that they wanted the restriction to last until 9pm. There weren't any traffic problems after 7pm so it can only have been about making money. What was ever wrong with transparency and clear signage? Well that is easy to answer. If everyone knew the rules, no one would park illegally and the councils wouldn't make money.

All this happened when they introduced red zones. They started to paint red lines on some of the major traffic arteries in place of the yellow ones that everyone was used to. They tested this out first to see if the system worked. To do this, they put red lines at roundabouts and other places where no one ever parked anyway. They left it for a couple of months and then declared it successful as no one was parking on the red lines. Doh! This meant that they could extend the scheme to all sorts of other roads. Roads where there were no parking issues like the dual carriageway outside my house. No one ever parked as there was a raised hard shoulder with unrestricted parking access. What they then did was to add loading bays in the carriageway so that lorries and vans could stop to unload. The effect of this was that where there was a road with no vehicles stopping for any reason, suddenly you had lorries blocking the lanes and causing tail backs, people changing lanes suddenly and cars coming out of parking spaces to be confronted with massive obstructions. These red lines were to be enforced by the traffic wardens of old. They no longer dealt with Yellow lines as the local councils had taken over that responsibility. So their job was to ensure that these main arteries were flowing. I've never seen a traffic warden from that day to this on any patrol or dishing out any tickets anywhere.

Wheel Clamping

Now here is the thing. There are all sorts of laws telling us where to park, how to park and when to park. When we breach these laws, the authorities are basically saying, "I don't want your car parked there. It is causing an issue in its current position." That's fair enough. It may be a hazard. It may just be causing the road to be congested. It may be as simple as the fact that your car is parked on a meter where other people who are willing to pay the fee are prevented from parking. As much as we hate these laws, they are there for a reason. But then, when they find your car breaching their laws, they go and throw a wheel clamp on to ensure your car is where they don't want it to be for an extra 3 hours. How is that sensible? When it is a private company, I think it is tantamount to extortion. "I have your car and I am going to keep it unless you give me money."

Scooters

This I find strangely interesting. Recently there has been a surge in the sales of scooters with small electric motors. These are like the kids scooters that we all scraped our knees and elbows on as youngsters in the 60s and 70s. They all but disappeared for a few years, came back looking a little different with much smaller skateboard wheels on them that kids used to break their legs and arms rather than the little scrapes we got ourselves into. They then disappeared again and now, all of a sudden, they are all grown-up modes of transport.

The government started to get their knickers in a twist about it until it seems, they tried to apply common sense. The problem was that they were illegal in terms of the Road Traffic Act (RTA). So they couldn't just ignore it. But they are environmentally friendly and didn't cause traffic jams so they wanted to encourage their use.

Why? I hear you ask. Exactly what is the problem? Well, the RTA has a load of rules and regs relating to motor vehicles. They are all about insurance, MOT tests to make sure they are road worthy, what one does in an accident and all that sort of stuff. The main issue is that to drive a motor vehicle on a road in the UK you need a driver's license, MOT and insurance. A 'motor vehicle', without going into too much boring rubbish, is defined as a mechanically propelled vehicle as opposed to 'vehicles' that include bicycles, skateboards, skis and so on. They didn't want to get Mr and Mrs 95 year old mobility vehicle user caught in this web so they added that the vehicle shouldn't be capable of doing over 5 miles an hour – walking speed plus a little bit.

Driving is described as having control of the speed and direction of a vehicle. So these scooters are mechanically propelled. They are buzzing down the road at 10 to 15 miles an hour and sometimes much more. By definition, a motor vehicle. How many people are getting insurance and MOTs for these vehicles? Well, it's a nice round figure at least.

A bicycle doesn't fit this definition because although it may be propelled using mechanics and it does go faster that 5 miles an hour (Unless my wife is doing the cycling), the power comes from your legs and not an outside source.

So the police are aware that they are illegal and are aware that if someone gets hurt using one of these things, all sorts of breast beaters will be getting onto their high horses and asking why the police ignored flagrant breaches of clear laws. I know of some actual issues caused by bad driving of these things. They seem to harass pedestrians on footways by weaving in and out, it is annoying but it isn't a big problem. So the government want to simply partially legalised them. I don't know how they would word it. I just like that idea that common sense has been attempted where it seldom does. In the meantime. The TV has been full of authorities telling us that they are illegal and can only be used on private land unless properly documented. They then follow this almost immediately by adverts selling the things as modes of transport.

speed

I need to say something about speed. A speed limit is just that. It is not a target, it is just the maximum speed at which you are allowed to travel. If the weather conditions are such that you can't see more than a dozen meters ahead, slow down to an appropriate speed. I have heard of emergency vehicles on blue light runs on motorways going at 50 mph to deal with pile-ups – caused by bad driving in foggy conditions – and seeing motorists overtaking them. They don't have to chase after them to give them words of advice, they just tell them about it after they have arrived at the pile-up and extricated them from the mangle that was their car five minutes earlier.

Having said that, if the conditions are clear, go at the speed limit. You may not be in a situation where tight schedules and time sensitive situations are a fact of life, but that doesn't mean that the half dozen cars behind you aren't full of drivers with those concerns. Have a care about others on the road and drive to the conditions. Speed doesn't kill, crashing does. Don't do it.

Use of car horns

I like that in British towns and cities, car horns are used much less than anywhere else in the world that I have experienced. I hardly ever use my car horn. There have been a number of occasions when I have needed to use it and had to look down to see where I had to press because, having never used it, I just didn't know. The thing is that a car horn does nothing but make a noise, it does not help to change speed or direction. The only way to extricate oneself from a hazardous situation is to change course or slow down. If you are approaching someone who is acting like an idiot, be they drivers, riders or pedestrians, pressing a horn only alerts them to your presence. If they are not of a mind to alter their behaviour, then it is down to you and ploughing on through them is not a good option. If it is a dangerous situation, then the brake pedal and steering are the best bet and these are not found at the centre of the steering wheel. Most people seem to use their horn as a way to swear at other road users. This isn't helpful. The horn is specifically there to warn other road users that your presence is hazardous to them (to put it another way, to warn them that you are a danger on the road). It is not there to tell the world that you are unhappy with another road users. Quite often, the regular users of horns are the problem in any case.

Odds and Sods

This could be considered the 'any other news' section. It is the chapter in which I will dump all the stuff that either doesn't fit a category or does but there is insufficient material to assign it an entire chapter.

Guns

Do I want to see the UK Police generally armed?

No.

So that has dealt with that subject.

There are police officers out there who I wouldn't trust with a pop gun much less a real one. There seem to be some officers who are forever having to submit their tasers or their pepper spray because they have deployed them. There are also others who hardly ever have to. I would never even carry the pepper spray. I used to walk around with a truncheon. It was part of my appointments. I was required to carry it. I never used it. So if there are officers out there who seem to be getting themselves into situations that they can't get out of without using that kind of force, while others seem to be able to avoid the problems in the first place, I would suggest that it is the officer, not the situation that is problematic. And if those officers have problems with control, I wouldn't let them carry guns.

It used to be that some officers would be trained in the use of firearms and become authorised to use them. They never carried them around on a day-to-day basis, but if a situation came up, they would be able to go to the local station and sign a weapon out with all the appropriate rubber-stamping from senior officers. They would then be able to go and deal with the situation. As there were not that many firearms around the general population, it seemed to work. The only guns out there were owned by specific groups of people. Sportspeople, under strict controls. They had to licence each firearm and were only allowed a limited number of bullets. A small number of the criminal fraternity who only tended to use them on each other, and the very rare armed robbery. Some youngsters who think they are all grown-up and belong to gangs carry them as status symbols. The only other people were posh gits with shotguns that they used to go out and murder clay pigeons.

But it all changed in terms of arming police. Some senior officer needed a promotion, so they came up with a plan. An entire unit of officers whose sole job it was to deal with firearm incidents. On the surface, this sounds pretty good. A group of officers who can specialise in one discipline and become expert. But there is a yang to that yin. If a firearms incident was happening, it would last minutes if that. These people don't put out double-page ads in the Times to tell everyone all about their plan to turn the West End into a scene from a 1960s spaghetti western. So when it happens, the perpetrators then disappear within seconds. Our all-singing-all-dancing firearms experts are few and far between. There will often be two or three active vehicles in the entire Met. So when they are called, they are often ten miles away. Bear in mind that it is already too late when they are called, it seems that there is little point of them being there when they will never be on the scene in time other than by sheer chance.

I personally never carried a firearm. I never wanted to and would have walked away from the job if I was instructed so to do. The main reason for this is that if a police officer discharges a firearm, it's because there is a person out there who is causing an immediate threat to the life of the officer, or any other person. There is no such policy that suggests only shooting to wound. A wounded man can still pull a trigger and, if the situation has descended that far, then the only policy is to stop that person from carrying out his aims. Don't even consider shooting in the leg. That carries the femoral artery. There is no way back if that is breached. Unfortunately, whenever someone is shot, there is always a mummy in the background ready to provided teary interviews to the press telling the world that her murderous offspring was really a good person and would never have harmed anyone. The police, on the other hand, were just out to get him and they are the murderers. The result of this is that the officer, who was acting entirely for the safety of the public, then has to be dragged through all sorts of enquires, accused of what boils down to an allegation of murder. Shiny-arsed politicians will scrutinise every second of the incident in the comfort of their air-conditioned offices, decide that split-second decisions should have been thought through and other options considered. They would then demand action is taken against the violent officer. You can imagine the scene playing out in the minds of these idiots. "Excuse me, sir. I know you want to press that button to blow up the explosives you have strapped to your waist. Could you just hang on a few minutes while I read my manual and go through all my options? I'd hate to blow you're brains out when there could have been other options available." I can see that happening. What these officers actually need is support. Not some political idiot trying to gain fame by criticising people for doing their job in highly charged situations. I was never going to put myself in that position. If I thought I would be supported, I might have considered it. That is pie in the sky.

They are obviously useful when there is going to be a planned raid on an address where they suspect firearms or when the shadowy world of the undercover cop reveals someone is out and about with a firearm. It means that they can be called in before any incident occurs. But these are rare occurrences. I only used this unit once in my 30-year career. For me, it was great. I just told them what I needed, gave them all the intel and they did the rest. I just stood back and became an observer until it was all over. I could then step in and do my Columbo impression. But to have an entire unit dedicated to this one discipline seems a waste of manpower. We only have to be aware that the media are all over it like a cheap suit every time a police firearm is discharged then count how many times we have read or heard reports on the news on this subject. It is rare.

Firearms legislation is a thing to behold. You can't own a gun. If you are a sportsperson, then the firearms have to be held in a secure place at a firearms club. Any firearm in a private house has to be locked in a safe that is attached to a structural part of the house. It has to be out of view and locked. Every weapon has to be registered; every round purchased has to be recorded. If you are transporting it, it has to be in a locked safe that is attached to the chassis of the vehicle you are in and out of sight. All good, no one needs guns. You only need to protect yourself from gun-wielding thugs if you are in that world anyway. I doubt that you are going to bother with registering your weapons if that is the case.

Shotguns are different. They are more lethal than many firearms but, because they are owned by landowners and toffs – you know, the ones that make the laws – the regulations are much more relaxed. You don't have to register each individual weapon. You don't have to register each purchase of cartridges. The age restriction is 15 as opposed to 18 for other firearms. The only thing that is absolute is that the length of the barrel is restricted to no less than 24". So no sawn-offs. Not allowed.

Pepper spray or other equivalent incapacitants are classified under Section 5 of the Firearms Act (FA) as a firearm. A bit weird but, because the FA describes firearms in a specific way, these items fall – somewhat vaguely – under this description. It was a bit off-putting because when we dealt with people on the street, we would often check to see if they had a criminal record. If they did, there would often be warning markers – one of which was 'firearms'. In the overwhelming majority of cases, this turned out to be pepper spray. It isn't pleasant, but it's hardly a saw-off shotgun.

You may also be glad to know that if a person has been sentenced to more than 5 years in prison, he is not allowed to own a gun. Those people must have sleepless nights worrying about not being armed because it is illegal.

I have no issue with banning all firearms outright. They are only used for hunting animals – which we don't need to do because we have farms – and hurting people. So why have them? Sport? I know sport is a little pointless and all about entertainment, but I see little of that in someone murdering a paper target at 100 yards. Sport is the manifestation of a metaphor for people playing out war and hunting scenarios. Aiming at a fixed target doesn't seem to cover any of those aims. Hey, it's only my opinion, some people even actually like football! Each to his own.

Pawn Shops

These are a protected species. I'm not sure why – they aren't endangered in any way. Especially in this day and age. So, you are wandering down the road without a care in the world wondering what's for dinner tonight. You walk past a shop with an item of property that you recognise as having been recently stolen from you. You can prove this and want it back. This should be possible. If the shopkeeper is of a mind, you may have to go through the courts, but if it can be proved that you own it and it was stolen, the law will often come down on your side. Unless it is a Pawnbroker. The law protects them. As long as they can show that they ensured that the seller had proprietary rights to the item, then those rights transfer absolutely to them when the deal is done.

So Harry Housebreaker comes into his local pawnbroker:

"Hello Harry, what do we have here?"

"It's my telly. I need some cash what can you give me for it?"

"Are you sure it is yours"

"Of course Guv, I've had it years, got it off my old granny when she passed."

"How many grannies do you have? This is the third telly this week!"

"Honest, guv, on my Grannies life, this is mine, have I ever lied to you?"

"Oh, all right, you can have a tenner for it."

"Thanks, guv."

If you then spot the telly for sale in the pawnbroker's shop, the likelihood is that they will not have to part with it without him getting something in exchange. There are codes-of-practice. They need to comply with certain standards, but it is the way of the world that some people are comfortable sailing close to the wind. They will do what is necessary and nothing more.

Mummy and Daddy come into the station to report a theft of their property and the fact that their daughter's shady boyfriend is the prime suspect. Compelling evidence is passed to me showing that the villainous boy is indeed prime suspect. He is arrested and interviewed and says it was his "bruvver wot dun it". I investigated and am just about coming to the conclusion that the parents are spot on when daughter arrives unannounced at the station. She wants to be interviewed about the incident. In the interview that followed, she stated that it was she who stole the property and gave it to her boyfriend. He was then to take it to a pawnbroker so that they could get some cash. It all seemed to fit. She answered all the questions. It seemed reasonable that the boyfriend would never have known of the property unless he was told. So she is now a prime suspect in a joint venture. The parents want the boy prosecuted to the full extent of the law. They will not agree to a prosecution of the daughter. I inform them that they have a choice. It had to be all or nothing. I cannot go to court and suggest to the judge that they ignore half the evidence. If I prosecute, they both go down. If the daughter isn't to be involved, then he won't be charged. Simple.

They reluctantly accept this but then go on to say that they want their property back. The pawnbroker has already been informed of the proceedings. They have kept hold of the property as per my requirements. They told me that they have a room full to overflowing with other property involved in police investigations. The police never get back to them when the case is over and they are stuck with it. They ask that I keep them updated. I inform the parents of the law surrounding the property.

Now here it seems to me that there is an easy way out. Their daughter was involved in the theft. All she has to do is go to the pawnbroker and pay the money back. They then get their property back. Easy? Of course not. The parents just want their property back and they don't see why they should pay. They complain to a DI who was an idiot who didn't know the law. He instructed me to seize the property and give it back to the parents. I sought advice and was told in no uncertain terms that if I complied with that instruction, I would be breaking the law. So I refused and informed the couple that if they weren't prepared to do the obvious thing, they would not get their property back. They only had a limited time to make their decision as the pawnbrokers would have to be informed that the investigation was complete. This would have released them from their obligations.

I don't particularly like the law surrounding this. It seems patently unfair to genuine owners who have lost what is rightfully theirs. But on this occasion, the law worked quite well.

Age-related issues

5 years

You are not allowed to feed anyone below this age alcohol. It's illegal, don't do it

10 years

The age of criminal responsibility. If you witness a 9-year-old stab someone to death, it should be obvious that you don't just shrug your shoulders and say, "Oh well, nothing we can do here, the child is below the age of criminal responsibility". Something would have to be done, just not through the judicial system. I do think that children of this age know a lot more than the law suggests although I do not believe that the judicial system is where one should deal with these issues.

12 years

Below this age, you cannot consent to sex. Anyone who does have sex with anyone under 12 is a rapist. It becomes complicated when both parties are below 12, but this is something that is normally dealt with outside the judicial arena. Below this age, the law insists that a person is not sufficiently aware of the full implications of sex and it's consequences to give proper informed consent.

Above this age, while the law realises that a person becomes more cognizant of the issues and can, therefore, give consent, they are just not allowed to until they are 16. The effect of this is that two people caught in flagrante delicto, both between 13 and 16 will probably be dealt with outside the judicial arena.

The main issue with this is a thorny one for which there is no satisfactory answer. Once a person becomes sexually active, they are usually sexually active for life from that point regardless of their age. (Of course, this does not include non-consensual sexual activity, a child who is forced into this is not sexually active for these purposes). Your body has no interest in laws, only urges. So when a parent becomes aware that their offspring is having sex before they have attained this age, what do they do about it? Ban them outright and tell them that they mustn't do it? That doesn't work. All that happens is they find inappropriate places, and possibly inappropriate people, to help them to sate their urges. But the parents can't legally just accept it and allow them to continue in a safe environment like their own home because they will be breaking the law as well. And don't believe for one moment that boys are worse than girls at this age. If your hormones are raging, there's nothing you can do and gender does not come into it.

14 years

Doli Incapax was, until the Crime and Disorder Act of 1998, a defence for a child between the age of 10 and 14, that they could not form criminal intent. It was the duty of the prosecuting authority to confirm that the person did have the capacity, normally through a few set questions. I'm glad they chucked it. If a child above the age of ten is not aware of right and wrong and what those consequences are, then the parents should be barred from ever having children.

15 years

The age at which one can possess a shotgun. That's scary!

16 years

Things change here. This is the age at which you can ride a moped.

It is also the age at which you can – subject to rules set by owners and managers – go into a pub. You can't drink anything alcoholic, but you can go in there.

It is also the age at which you can drink beer, cider, perry or Wine in a restaurant with a proper, sit-down meal. You can't go into a restaurant area of a pub, buy a bag of crisps and drink yourself into oblivion. It doesn't work like that.

It is also the age at which you can enjoy the charms of the opposite sex, at least for people like me. Those that enjoy same-sex relationships are also released from any and all non-parental restrictions.

It was also the age at which I could legally drive as I was a resident of Zimbabwe. Their rules are different.

So this is the first time you can legally drive and go to the pub. That's also scary!

17 years

The age at which you can drive a car, van or motorcycle in the UK.

18 years

The world is your oyster. You are a big grown-up, sensible, ready to take on life by the scruff-of-the-neck. Yeah, right!

Now, going through these ages, you may notice a huge gap when considering alcohol use. You can't feed a person under 5, alcohol and you can purchase and drink alcohol – with strict caveats in place – at 16. There is a void between these ages. There are few pieces of legislation governing what a person can and can't do with alcohol. You can't go into a pub. You can't drink alcohol in licensed premises, you can't buy alcohol and you can't purchase alcohol for people under 18 except in a restaurant. But there is nothing to say you can't walk down the road at the age of 6 swigging on a bottle of gut-rot whisky. Clearly, right-minded people are not just going to ignore it, and things should be done. Just not through judicial processes.

So the legal age for alcohol in this country is 5. At least when I last read the law. It may have changed.

Harassment

This is a piece of legislation that has a lot in common with the Public Order Act. That act was there to deal with immediate single issues involving disturbances and general problem stirring. The Harassment act was there to deal with ongoing and persistent issues. In brief there as to be a series of similar actions that the perpetrator knows, or should know, causes harassment, alarm and/or distress to an individual or group of people. It can take many forms from what we have come to recognise as stalking all the way down to neighbours getting under each other's skins. Even though there has to be evidence of an ongoing and persistent issue, no time scale is attached. You can have a person consistently phoning a victim at 3am every night. You can have the same person making dozens of phone calls in the same night, or it can be someone who does something once a year on an anniversary of whatever it is the person has an issue with. All we need to show is a series of actions that causes someone to be harassed or frightened in some way.

The problems came about because politicians felt the need to keep tweaking the policies surrounding this. Much of this is linked with domestic issues, so policy-makers were always running scared instead of just dealing with it. The law is quite straight forward. If you follow it, it works quite well. If we take a typical example of a bloke hassling a woman with whom he has designs. She tells him to 'go forth and multiply' but he can't take a hint and continues. Now this, on the surface of it, is the complete offence. But only if the woman is feeling threatened or harassed. The law, of course, wants the i's dotted and the t's crossed so, even in these circumstances, he is spoken to by police. He claims that he's only larking around and didn't think he was causing any harm. Police officers should then tell him that is actions are causing problems and, if it continues, he will be in breach of the Harassment Act. What this does is take away any future defence that he thought he wasn't causing problems. It is all recorded. He has nowhere to go.

This is all very well until you get an issue where the harassment is overtly problematic and cannot be excused away. Politicians like to lump everything into categories. At first, they insisted that in all cases the person causing the problem had to be given an 'official police warning'. Which is fine if there was any such thing in this format. Official police warnings are only dished out when an offence has been committed, admitted to and signed off by the offender. This goes on the Police National Computer (PNC) and is treated in a similar way to a conviction. Some detective having a word in someone's shell-like appendage and telling him to 'wind his neck in' isn't going to cut it. It is perfectly good evidence – if recorded – to take away the defence that they thought they were not causing a problem, but there is little official about it. They then decided to start serving written notifications on these people and getting them to sign the paperwork to the effect that they had been warned. Again this is all fine and is evidence that takes away the defence, but there is little in the way of law that supports this as an official way to deal with it. The offender has no obligation to sign anything. When the police found out that it had no legal backing, they just ceased doing it, insisting that it was not worth the paper it was written on. It seemed that they just didn't get it. Any written document can be evidence if used in the right way.

In addition to this, it doesn't deal with the issues of the really violent person who, up to that point, hasn't done anything more than harass the victim, but intel suggests a predilection towards violence if his voice isn't heard. The last thing the police should be doing to waiting for him to strike before taking action. The whole point of the act was to prevent that escalation. There is also the issue that, in telling the suspect that the victim has got the police involved may well exacerbate any problems rather than solving them. People who have violent tendencies do not tend to switch them off just because the police tell them to.

The way it is dealt with is easily resolved by taking each incident on its own merit and not compartmentalising it as a single issue. If a person is causing problems, has been made aware of this to a standard allowed by law, and continues regardless, then they have committed the offence. If it is low-level stuff, give them every opportunity to mend their ways without resorting to the courts. If the person is known to be dangerous, take appropriate measures by arresting if the evidence is there. If it isn't, protect the victim until the evidence is properly gathered. If the person has not been made aware of their actions being problematic, make them aware. If the issue is obviously causing problems to any reasonable person, and there are a series of actions that show this to be potentially dangerous, dispense with the warnings and let them explain to the court why they are being idiots.

This stuff is dealt with by police as a low-level crime. The hurt and anxiety it causes to the victim is huge, and sometimes overwhelming. It affects all parts of our society equally. No one is immune. The internet has provided a different way for perpetrators to continue causing these problems. This only heightens the issue because the person being harassed can be got to anywhere at any time. I had a colleague who was being stalked by a woman to the point that she even accosted him while he was on duty, in uniform, doing CPR on the victim of a road accident. She actually had to be dragged away so that he could attend to the victim. She was being fed information from someone within the station. When she realised that he had decided to take a six-month sabbatical, she threatened to make a complaint against him in order to scupper his pans. (any serious complaint has to be dealt with before anyone takes a substantial amount of time off and their leave application will be put on hold for the duration of the investigation). He dealt with this by telling everyone except for me, a sergeant and the senior management, that he intended to go in mid-August then slipped away a month earlier before she had the opportunity to make her complaint. There were a few stunned faces at the station, but she disappeared into obscurity and, to my knowledge, never caused him an issue again. Such are the lengths one has to go through to diminish the effects of these offenders.

And Finally

So, there we have it. We have a bunch of laws created by people who have no vested interest in making them effective. They are practised by people who have a vested interest in finding holes in them. They are enforced by people who are pulled hither and thither by the above-mentioned characters for reasons of politics and personal gain. This is all to control a population who, for the most part, don't need to be controlled.

There aren't any answers. Despite all the issues, the system seems to get by. Throw in a load of common sense for those who are given the task of enforcing legislation. Understand that the population at large are people who comply with these laws without ever knowing the intricacies or even the basics of some of them, and you have a system that does sort of work.

Don't kill people – Murder.

Don't hurt people – offences against the person Act and rape.

Don't Nick stuff – The Theft Act.

Have a little respect for other people's property – Criminal Damage Act

Be decent – Public Order Act.

Lend a hand to people who truly need it regardless of who they are – Common decency.

And a plethora of other laws telling people they are not allowed to do things that most don't want to do anyway.

My advice to coppers just starting out in the detective arena is keep it simple. Juries are every-day people. Some are intelligent, some not so, most are somewhere in the middle. But they all have an agenda that does not always follow the legal script. Always remember that you can't prove a negative, so your evidence has to be what you can prove happened not what you or they can't. So keep it simple and concentrate on the one or two pieces of evidence that are irrefutable and present it in a package wrapped in all the other irrelevant rubbish that politicians, CPS, defence teams et al are so insistent that they have. Investigate everything whether it supports the case or not and disclose everything, especially the bits that cast doubt. If you can find it, so can they and it can be embarrassing when they produce evidence that you know about but have said you didn't. Be honest.

I worked with a guy who always seemed to charge a lot of people as a result of his investigations. He was evidently good at getting to the truth. What he was not so good at was prioritising the bits that could not be denied or ignored. So he would be going to court with boxes upon boxes of exhibits and paperwork. He used to take over entire storerooms for the duration of the trials. They would go on for weeks on end and normally end up in acquittal. I, on the other hand, would roll up to court with all my paperwork in a single ring binder file. My trials seldom made it to a second week and 75% of them ended in conviction. It wasn't because I was better or worse than him. It was because I kept it simple.

Here are some examples to illustrate this point.

The lady who was raped by someone who she thought was a friend: She said rape, he said consensual sex, the 999 recording and signs of a struggle where he had to force her trousers down, said otherwise.

The Lady whose uncle sexually attacked her trying to hide behind her mental difficulties: She said rape, he said sex didn't happen at all. Semen stains on the sheet said otherwise.

The young girl who was attacked in a park by 5 boys who had lured her in there on the pretence of helping her out at around midnight in February: She said multiple rapes, the boys variously said either that it was consensual or it didn't happen. The occupant of the random address she knocked on – because she saw lights from within – while she was semi-naked, dishevelled, confused, crying and injured, kind of told it's own story. The condom wrapper complete with fingerprints confirmed the incident took place. The 'cut-throat defence' was the icing on the cake.

The disturbance outside a nightclub: The punter said that the doormen were over the top in their methods. The doormen said they were trying to quell a potentially violent situation. CCTV said the doormen were lying.

Don't be afraid to deal with the one elephant in the room that everyone seems to try to avoid. The question 'why'. How many times have I heard someone saying, "He hit me for no reason", or "I was just minding my own business and he just came up to me and started swearing at me." It doesn't happen. Unless there are mental issues involved, there is almost invariably a reason. No one does anything without some kind of a trigger. If the person has committed a crime that could land them in prison, you can bet that there is one and if you dig deep enough, you'll find it. Look for the 'why', because if you find that, you will normally get to the bottom of what you are investigating. The only caveat is that you can't physically ask the question because you will never get the truthful answer. You can only do it through investigation.

The majority of cases that go to trial do so because the defence team believe there are chinks in the evidence. If there wasn't, the defendant would be advised appropriately. So court cases are never cut and dried. However, I did not take anything to trial unless I was convinced of the truth. It meant that any 'chinks' could, more often than not, be explained. The evidence I could then present to the court revealed the truth. You don't need a month-long trial to get this across. You only need to tell the story and introduce the evidence that confirms it. Defence barristers would love to make it complicated. Don't pander to it. Don't give them the opportunity.

There are no mysteries in this. Just make sure the one Law you never breach is tax laws. The government and the judiciary can forgive a lot in our shiny new world, but tax evasion is unforgivable on any level – unless you are a politician, of course, then it is de rigueur.

Epilogue

I am now happily retired. I am waiting for my sons to become fabulously wealthy so that I can live a life to which I am willing to become accustomed. I know I will never be wealthy. I am not acquisitive enough. I spend my time writing, playing my various musical instruments, painting and drawing for my own pleasure, cooking for me and my wife who has had to put up with me for 40 years so it's the least I can do. I also quite enjoy winding up my middle-aged German lodger who seems to dislike following me around mopping up after me but does it of her own accord anyway.

This is my second literary rant and perhaps not my last. I still have loads of ideas swishing around my head.

If I get bored with writing, or playing, or cooking, or whatever else I decide to turn my hand to, my wife and I jump into the motorhome. We like to go out looking for interesting walks in the countryside invariably ending up in one of the many cosy Micropubs that are proliferating through the length and breadth of Great Britain. I wonder, could that be my next subject? Watch this space.

Acknowledgements

While I haven't given credit to the good work of specific individuals in this monologue, nor have I outed anyone for the bad stuff. For the most part, this is so that I do not fall foul of the Data Protection Act. Suffice to say, the individuals involved may well recognise themselves if they were to read this but probably no one else. Those who do good know it and should be rightly proud. Those who have fallen short, please learn from the mistakes.

I need to pay tribute to one individual, Tess McCarthy, who has given up her time and extensive legal knowledge to copy-edit this into something readable. Without her insights and good grammar, I would be lost

Made in the USA
Middletown, DE
27 February 2024

50477012R00104